Signed $3.00

Margaret Vaughn

a True
Friend

Jenny Buchanan
30 March '07

MY CONVERSATIONS WITH GOD

Wondering, Pondering and Trying to Get It Right

BY
HENRY A. BUCHANAN

Bloomington, IN  Milton Keynes, UK

AuthorHouse™
1663 Liberty Drive, Suite 200
Bloomington, IN 47403
www.authorhouse.com
Phone: 1-800-839-8640

AuthorHouse™ *UK Ltd.*
500 Avebury Boulevard
Central Milton Keynes, MK9 2BE
www.authorhouse.co.uk
Phone: 08001974150

© *2007 Henry A. Buchanan. All rights reserved.*

No part of this book may be reproduced, stored in a retrieval system, or transmitted by any means without the written permission of the author.

First published by AuthorHouse 1/25/2007

ISBN: 978-1-4259-7685-9 (sc)
ISBN: 978-1-4259-7686-6 (hc)

Printed in the United States of America
Bloomington, Indiana

This book is printed on acid-free paper.

Contents

PREFACE ix

CHAPTER ONE
About Adam and Eve in the Garden 1

CHAPTER TWO
About the Tower of Babel 7

CHAPTER THREE
The Rest of the Story About the Flood 11

CHAPTER FOUR
About That Pillar of Salt 19

CHAPTER FIVE
About Abraham 24

CHAPTER SIX
About Jacob 32

CHAPTER SEVEN
About Joseph 36

CHAPTER EIGHT
About Moses 43

CHAPTER NINE
About That Damn Goat 50

CHAPTER TEN
About Joshua and the Walls of Jericho 58

CHAPTER ELEVEN
About Old Samuel   64

CHAPTER TWELVE
About Saul the First King   71

CHAPTER THIRTEEN
About Solomon   76

CHAPTER FOURTEEN
About Amos and Micah Too   82

CHAPTER FIFTEEN
About Balaam's Ass   87

CHAPTER SIXTEEN
About Samson   93

CHAPTER SEVENTEEN
About Esther the Queen   96

CHAPTER EIGHTEEN
About Daniel   99

CHAPTER NINETEEN
About Elijah/Elisha   104

CHAPTER TWENTY
About Job   110

CHAPTER TWENTY ONE
About Jonah and the Fish   116

CHAPTER TWENTY TWO
About John the Baptist   123

CHAPTER TWENTY THREE
About Jesus the Christ — 128

CHAPTER TWENTY FOUR
About the Third Day — 137

CHAPTER TWENTY FIVE
About Judas — 143

CHAPTER TWENTY SIX
About Peter — 149

CHAPTER TWENTY SEVEN
About Paul the Apostle — 154

CHAPTER TWENTY EIGHT
About the Lost Letters (a Fiction) — 160

CHAPTER TWENTY NINE
About Harlots & Fallen Women — 175

CHAPTER THIRTY
About David — 179

CHAPTER THIRTY ONE
The Creation Myth and the Rise of Man — 186

EPILOGUE — 199

PREFACE

To My Conversations with God

Bible Stories. Biblical Heroes. They are the bone structure of The Story itself. When I was a boy I thrilled to the high adventure of David and Daniel, and of Peter and Jesus. I talked with God about the people and the adventures of MY own life. He had spoken to me and given me a role in the great unfolding drama of the twentieth century. It was not all clear and I wondered.

As a young man I embraced that adventure. Sometimes with more courage than wisdom, but always with a sense of excitement at the discovery of His purpose in the world. As a mature man I found my role hand in hand with my suffering but hoping fellows grappling with the issues of life.

Now I am old, and I no longer run the footrace of youth. Neither do I wrestle with the giants of the Earth in mortal combat for what is right. But in quietness I talk with God Who is always directing my thoughts to the great men who have fashioned the Faith by which I live. And still it is a wondering experience, and I write the story we both have shared. That is the way these conversations with God came to be written.

For I believe that beneath and inside these briefly told tales in the Bible, God has hidden His Truth amidst both humor and wit, to encourage me in MY struggle of faith. And these are living tales that are ever generating new life out of the living experience of man on Earth. So I held this wondering conversation with God about all these people and happenings, and I was as surprised as you will be at what I have written here.

So I give you here MY CONVERSATIONS WITH GOD about the Story in the Book, starting with the Creation, I walked on the mountain tops Out of Eden.

I was going to wind up with the dramatic Apocalypse of John, but God warned me against deep waters and to stay clear of the treacherous path already trodden by misguided enthusiasts and just plain fools. He said to me "You want a mystery for your own day? You will find it in the struggles of brave and desperate men who have found their own role models, good and bad, in My Book. Write. For I have spoken to you, even as I have spoken to faithful man through the ages. And mind you, a little humor, a smidgen of wit, and not so much of the heavy preaching you did in Shellman. But get it right. And tell it right."

CHAPTER ONE

About Adam and Eve in the Garden

It may seem strange to you, Patient Reader, that after I have sought the deep meaning of those Three Days in the tomb of Jesus, I would revert to the story of Adam and Eve in the Garden of Eden. Why? you will ask me, go backward in time when God has given to His Church a forward vision that will carry it to the conquest of the world? Simply because, with all the Light that has been thrown on the Way, the Church continues to ignore what really happened back there in Eden.

What I mean to tell you here is that while the Church has been talking about Original Sin and the guilt of Adam and Eve, the really important part of the story has lain hidden in the Mind of God for all these thousands of years, and I, the ever inquisitive Seeker after Truth, dared to run where angels feared to tread. I just asked God: "What did Adam and Eve say to one another when they got this order from You about lording it over the creation and tending the Garden and staying clear of the Tree of the Knowledge of Good and Evil?"

You may be quite surprised to learn that God was willing to hear my question and give me the background on that event which marks the Great Divide in Man's life. He even seemed pleased that I had asked, and He commented that one of the great disappointments that He has experienced in trying to make something worth while out of the

Man He had created was that nobody had ever asked. He said "the preachers and so called theologians have seemed satisfied with those few lines in the Creation story, and they have not seemed interested in knowing any more. But you now, just what is it that you want to know?"

"Like I said, I want to know about the conversation between Adam and Eve before, during and after they ate that fruit people insist that it was an apple of the tree of the Knowledge of Good and Evil? It's not like a woman just to do something that is going to have an effect on the whole human race and not even say a word about it to her husband, which is what I assume she called Adam. And what did Adam say to Eve when she said what she said to him about eating the ap ... er fruit. We are told what Adam said to God when he had been caught, and we know that what a man says to God is not necessarily what he says to his wife when he is about to do something that will alter the course of human history.

"In fact, it seems to me that the Serpent - surprise, surprise, a snake talking - is the main spokesman here, and although I have a keen interest in snakes, and not necessarily a favorable one, I would like to know more about that snake's role in this little drama. How did he know so much about God and Man, and the secret of Good and Evil?"

God said "You must have been making a whole list of questions. And you keep on rolling them out as if you are afraid you will forget one of them. But I will try to enlighten you, since you do seem to be a rare bird, by which I mean that you are asking the right questions.

"Now let's take Adam and Eve first. They are husband and wife, and you too have been married a couple of times. In fact, you have spent better than a half century in wedlock, so you are right in your perception that the business of the fruit did not take place in silence. In fact, it all started when Eve came home from a solitary walk in the Garden, and she opened up the subject by saying to Adam. I met the most interesting character today. Of course, Adam's natural curiosity drove him to ask Who? although you know that husbands' response to wives reports of this nature are not always genuine since they expect it to be some idle gossip of a trivial nature.

But Eve said He called himself The Serpent, and Adam came right back at her and said He called himself the Serpent? I will have you know that I am the one who told him that was his name. That was before you even put in your appearance on the scene."

"But Eve would not be put off by Adam's superiority act, and she said He, the serpent, was impressive. In fact, he was the most intelligent creature, with the exception of you, of course, whom I have met in my walks in the Garden. Subtle is the word for him, I guess."

Adam was placated by being put above the Serpent in Eve's list of intelligent beings, so he wanted to know more about this meeting between Eve and the serpent. "So what did you talk about that gave you the impression that he was intelligent?"

"Well, he raised a question about our Freedom. Or you might just say, How much control do we really have here in the Garden?"

"This certainly got Adam's attention because be thought he was in control of everything, based on what I had said to him about dominion and he had forgotten, apparently, that one exception And it was this chink in his armor which the Serpent's tongue had found, and now his wife was exploring. For Eve had been listening when I said it. She had memorized it and now she repeated not only what I had said, but the Serpent's comment on it."

"Seems to me," I said, wanting to appear knowledgeable, "that the one exception was the fruit of the Tree of the Knowledge of Good and Evil."

"You are right. And that Serpent gave away My secret because that is the key to everything. To know both Good and Evil would make Adam just like Me and not a mere image of Me. The Reality rather than a Reflection. He would be truly Man full grown and not merely an innocent child. He would be grown up."

"Sounds like potent stuff too, in view of what Man has been able to do since he discovered fire and the wheel and writing and ..."

"Those things are impressive, but the real thing is that Knowledge of Good and Evil. This implies the ability to act with mature judgment and awareness of the consequences of one's own action."

"I see," I said, although I was not quite sure that I did see, but God was intent on getting me to see it all in the light of the conversation between Adam and Eve. "Adam now saw what was to be gained. You might say that he saw how this Woman I had given him could help him to become what he wanted to be, and when she held out to him the Fruit from the Tree of the Knowledge of Good and Evil, he took it eagerly, and he ate it, and he got his eyes opened, and what he saw scared him into hiding, and when I dragged him out into the open, he tried to lay the whole thing onto his wife Eve, and she passed it on to the Serpent. Now that's a quick rehash of what you have read a dozen times."

I agreed that I had read that part in the Bible story, but had missed any conversation between Adam and Even that might give me a clue to the real question which was: How much did they understand about what had happened to them when they ate the Fruit of the Tree of Knowledge of Good and Evil, and I continued to pursue this matter. I said, "Then what?"

"You don't need a verbatim account in order to get the message, but you can he sure that there was some whispering between the two of them because they would think I would not hear unless they spoke out, but the main concern was for the potential this fruit offered. Eve said "The Serpent seems to know what he is talking about. You would think he could see right into the mind of God. And you have to give him credit for being a pretty slick character who can renew his life just by shedding his old outgrown skin and coming out new again. Now if we had the secret we could live forever and there is no limit to what we could do."

"Adam saw it too, even though he was a bit slower than Eve, but once he saw it, there was no stopping him. Now he has that Knowledge, and he has done a lot of both Good and Evil with it."

I just stared open mouthed at God when he said the next thing. "And the best part of all is that this was just exactly what I wanted them to do."

"You did?"

"Of course. But by forbidding it, I made certain that they would get it, or bust."

"But what about the dying?"

"Oh yes, Adam brought that up and reminded Eve that I had told them that if they disobeyed and ate it anyway, they would die."

"Then you deceived them? Played a trick on them? A Trickster God like the ones Africans have?"

"No. Not that. Death was in the picture all along. Physical death. It begins at birth. Necessary. Without it we would have chaos and so much conflict between the generations that Life on Earth would be unbearable. They already had the Secret of renewing of life through procreation. But what died was the innocence and the ignorance and the irresponsibility of childhood. They became like Me, bearing the burden of moral responsibility for the world on their shoulders."

"So the Serpent was right. They just didn't see the whole picture?"

"Most people still don't. That's why they have to dream up an afterlife that's nothing more than a perpetual childhood."

"So what about your throwing them out of the Garden, and setting a flaming sword to prevent their reentrance. And all that work for Adam? And the labor of childbirth for Eve?"

"Figures of speech; don't forget that Speech was the supreme gift that I bestowed on them. If Man could not describe his misery, and his happiness, in Speech, he couldn't bear the one nor enjoy the other. But it is a figure of speech which does describe very well what happened. Do you think you can ever recapture the innocence of childhood? Do you think you can be carefree again? Do you think you can ever get back into the garden of childhood where somebody else pays the bills and you can run free at play? Those two were now grown ups and they would never be children again. But who would really want to be, if he thinks about it?"

"So all this talk I hear from the aspirants to high political office about the hard working people they represent and propose to set free from their labors ...?"

"Is just so much talk. They are pulling wool over your eyes. Work is Man's chief joy. His greatest happiness. His true medium. It is in his work that he truly finds himself, his Manhood."

"And the curse on Woman? The pangs of childbirth?"

"Curse? Don't believe it. If it were that bad, the single pair would not have increased to near six billion in so short a period of time. If it were all that bad, Sex would not be the favorite indoor sport that it is today."

"Well, I have to say that I never realized there could be so much meaning in such a short story. No wonder the writer had to tell it twice in a row. I guess he was just enjoying himself so much ..."

"That does not concern you. Just see that you get everything I have told you down on paper just the way I told it to you. There's your immortality."

CHAPTER TWO

ABOUT THE TOWER OF BABEL

After the terrorists hit the Twin Towers of the World Trade Building, and brought it all down, and just about wrecked the economy of the nation, to say nothing of how nobody on radio or TV could say anything without a reference to Nine Eleven, I asked God about that tall building out there in the middle of nowhere that was referred to in the Bible as the Tower of Babel.

I had pondered on the tale rather sketchily told there in Genesis, and I didn't know just what to make of it, for it was a mystery to me.

Then God said "You remember way back yonder when you were in the eighth grade and staying with Miss Florrie, and she made you study Latin?"

Of course I remembered it. "I hated it. But Miss Florrie was a lot like You. When she said to me You will study Latin, I knew I was going to study Latin because there was no getting out of it. But she explained it to me."

"She did indeed. And what was the explanation Miss Florrie gave you for studying Latin?"

"She said it would help me to speak English and any other language I might undertake to learn to speak."

"Well, think of that Tower of Babel, as it is called, as Latin in reverse."

"Now I am more confused than ever because I had trouble enough with Latin in forward gear. Now I have to fight Caesar's Gallic Wars backwards?"

I am lucky that God has a fine sense of humor, and that He is patient with me when I am testy. He said "Now that tale about the Tower. It is sometimes told to explain how it is that people in different parts of the world speak different languages, and they don't understand one another, and so they wind up shouting obscenities at one another, and hitting one another over the head with a club."

Now I was beginning to feel better about my own ignorance because I never did master Latin well enough to pray in Latin the way the Church Fathers did. And Greek. Once I thought I would show off my learning in the pulpit by reading the text in the Gospel from my Greek New Testament. The truth is that I had memorized the English version and when I came, to the part where I was to translate it for the benefit of the congregation, I just sailed right through it like I was reading from the King James.

"Cheating," God said. "Riding a pony the way you tried to do on Caesar's Gallic Wars."

"Caught again," I said, "but Hebrew was my nemesis, and I couldn't get past the first four words of the Ten Commandments. In fact, I dreaded Hebrew so much I put it off until my last year in Theological Seminary, hoping I might get hit by a truck and not have to take Hebrew."

"I was saving you for something though, and so I rerouted the truck traffic that had been passing the Seminary. Pulled the trucks off Lexington Road and sent them to Frankfort Avenue. But you were pondering, as you put it, what happened on that Tower. So what do you want to know about it?"

"The workmen. It must have been a nightmare for them. It's hard enough for me to follow directions spoken in English by a Yankee. Impossible with a Brit. Remember the time I was lost in Chicago and asking directions ..."

"Never mind Chicago. Those fellows building the Tower were an arrogant crew and it was their motive for doing that really ticked me off. They were going to ascend into heaven, take the place by storm and run the world from on high. Couldn't wait to live a decent, law abiding life of justice, mercy and humility, then go to heaven the right way. They were going to force the gates."

"So what happened when You decided to stop them?"

"It was bedlam. The mortar mixers couldn't get it right when the foreman tried to tell them how much mortar to prepare. They were always coming up with a shortage or a surplus. One evening at sunset they were closing down work and the mortar mixer had a truckload left over and the next morning it had set up hard.

"And the stonecutters couldn't understand where the foreman wanted the stones cut so they would fit in, and that's why the thing looks like a crazy man designed it. You would have laughed your head off at the paymaster when he tried to make up the payroll. He was paying out more for common labor than the skilled artisans were getting."

"That must have thrown things out of gear. When you mess with money."

"That was what finally brought the project to a halt. Everybody quit in a huff and went off home or to the beer joints. Those who went home found it impossible to talk with their wives, and the ones who went to the bars couldn't even order a beer because the bartender couldn't understand whether a fellow wanted a Miller Light or a Hudepohl. You understand, I hope, that I am using language here that is of your own time in the hope that it will be relevant to you."

"I was hoping that the ones who went home would fare better than the ones at the bars."

"It is not unusual for husband and wife to speak two different languages."

"So the great experiment ended in confusion. And did men then give up the dream of heaven?"

"Not at all. Only now they have a different scheme. If you have listened to any sermons lately, you ought to know what it is. But we are talking about the confusion of tongues. And that political campaign you are involved in right now ought to be a lesson to you. All the candidates are saying the same thing but the people listening to them are all hearing something different."

"Amazing, how modern that old Tower has become now that we have talked about it. So what's going to happen in Iraq where we have a language barrier to start with?"

"It's going to get worse. Because the Iraqis don't hear what you are saying, and you are not hearing what they are saying. Remember that document Saddam sent to your President. Written in Sanskit. And the President wasn't even reading the English translation."

"I have been wondering if they hear the same thing we hear when we talk to them about Freedom and Democracy."

"You might well wonder if the President means what you think those words mean."

"And what about Separation of Church and State?"

"Oh My Word. Neither one of you knows what you are talking about. You are building a twenty first century Tower of Babel ... But not to worry. A terrorist will knock it down...Or one of your tanks will do the job on it."

CHAPTER THREE

The Rest of the Story About the Flood

When I heard about how God had told Pat Robertson that George Bush is going to win by a landslide, I said Why can't God let me in on things? I am at least as deserving as Pat Robertson. And then I began to get these good vibes which might have been direct from heaven and a Voice said to me "I can't trust you with the future because you are too reckless, but I will tell you something about the past that will stand you on your ear. The reason I am doing this is that I know how interested you are in history as well as the mythology that goes for history and might as well be true because there is so much good stuff in it."

That sounded good enough for me because when you are dealing with God you take what you can get. I reasoned that if Pat Robertson had asked God the right question he might have got something more worthwhile than a political prognostication. So I said, seeing I might have a small bargaining point here, could I have a choice about what it is I want to know that happened in the past? And the Voice said "Why not? the past is past. What do you want to know?" I said "The Flood. The Big One. Noah's Flood. That's always been a big mystery to me. And mind You, I am not planning to climb Mount Ararat in search of the Ark But I would like to know about the day to day human events leading up to the Flood. About Noah's round up of all the livestock that went into that big boat. And feeding and cleaning up behind them all and, well ..."

But the Voice stopped me and said "One thing at a time and don't get ahead of yourself. I guess you would like to know about the conversation that went on between Noah and his wife, starting with when he announced at the supper table that he was going to build a big boat and he began giving her the dimensions and describe how he was going to make it waterproof and what she had to say."

So you can see that sometimes God knows more about what it is that I want to know than I do myself, so I said "Having been married a couple of times myself, I can imagine the boat building project must have sparked some lively dinnertime conversation." That was when I heard this loud guffaw that sounded like thunder more than anything else I can think of to describe it, and the Voice spoke again.

"Oh yes, Mrs. Noah, whom Noah was accustomed to refer to as The Old Woman, had some questions for Noah and some opinions to express about what seemed to be a hare brained project to undertake out there on the farm on dry ground. She pointed out to Noah that he had already shown a tendency to neglect the garden and the general upkeep of the house, and things were going to wrack and ruin while he sat around day dreaming, and now she knew what it was he was day dreaming about. It was some relief to her at first to learn that he was not day dreaming about a younger woman, but when she realized it was some project involving God, then she knew she was really against competition because when a religious idea gets hold on a man's brain, there is no stopping him."

But Noah was certain that he had heard God right. There was going to be a Big Flood and he, Noah, was instructed to build a Big Boat to cope with the Flood. So Noah said to his wife "Old Woman, the house and garden and the privy are all going to go when the Flood comes." Mrs. Noah was not to be quieted easily though and she said "The pigs. They've pushed up the rails and are running out of the pen, rooting up the potatoes and my flower beds and ..."

"But Noah said "Pigs. No future for pigs anyway. I'll save a pair because God has told me to save a pair of everything, but when Moses comes he will put the skids under pigs. Now you just attend to your work in the kitchen. Stop meddling."

Mrs. Noah gathered up the dishes and seemed to be inclined to grumble some more so Noah said "Me and the boys will build this boat, and we will have a little section for the pigs, but it's the giraffes that are giving me trouble. Head room is what I need for them. Tall fellows, the giraffes." He glanced around at the boys and said "Shem and Japheth are coming along well as boat builders. Ham is a bit slow but he can fetch and carry, and we will make out. Now you just mind your woman's work. In the kitchen. We are going to need a lot of food cooked up in advance to carry us through the Flood."

"Well now," the Voice said to me, "I don't have to go into a lot of detail about all the domestic issues that arise when I pick out a man to do a big job for me. You know how it is when a man and a woman get crosswise on things like paying the bills on time and making proper arrangement for the children's education and even for one's own funeral. So you can expect a few knock down drag out fights when a man has to make a decision about following My instructions and his wife does not see it that way. But I have to hand it to Noah. He put his foot down. He has a big foot too. In fact, some of his neighbors called him Big Foot. But he put his big foot down and he said to Mrs. Noah "I've got plenty of work for the boys to keep them busy. They've learned enough in school to do the measurements that I give them. Shem and Japheth anyway, and Ham can do the caulking, and that's more important than you may realize because when the water starts to rise we don't want it coming in through cracks in the boat."

"Mrs. Noah said something about the cracks in the old man's head and said it would take more than caulking to keep his brains from leaking out, if there were any left to leak out by the time he got his big boat built. "On dry land too," she reminded him, as if the neighbors had not already brought that to his mind.

A little hassle with 'the old woman' was just warmup for the tussle Noah was going to have loading all those animals. Domestic animals, no problem. Old Rover took to the Ark like a duck to water, and the Pussy Cat thought It was a place worth exploring, but the big cats, I mean lions and tigers and cougars, were not friendly to the idea of swapping the open spaces for cages, inside a boat. And that's to say nothing about the bears. If it had been winter time and they were hibernating, the bears would have been a pushover, but it was Springtime and there is nothing meaner than an old Mama Bear with Cubs unless it's an old Papa Bear with mating with Mama Bear on his mind. So Noah was having enough problems to make a preacher cuss, and all the jokes his neighbors were making up about him did not improve his disposition any.

"I reckon a nagging wife wasn't much help," I said, thinking back on my own domestic experiences, and the Voice said "Oh, Mrs. Noah had a word or two to say about some of those animals. It had never occurred to her that I had some purpose in mind when I created each one of them. She didn't like the skunks for the obvious reason, and Noah just would put them where the wild dogs could see them and this set the dogs off and of course all that barking got the skunks tails up, and you know what happens when a skunk raises his tail. I was on a roll when I created skunks.

"So suffice it to say that Noah had a rough time at the loading and the neighbors standing around hooting did not help at all. Nor did Mrs. Noah's questions about how he was going to feed all of those wild animals when he couldn't keep bread on the table for his family, what with wasting his time on this fool project. The kindest response that Noah made to his wife at that time was "You are not being helpful."

"Mrs. Noah went back to her work in the kitchen and Noah and his three sons went back to the boat. They were loading, storing the feed for the animals and trying to figure out how to keep the meat eaters from eating the herbivores the way they were accustomed to doing in the wild. Noah said "Boys, feeding is just the beginning of our work with all these critters. It's when we start to shoveling camel dung that we are going to be sweating. Just you wait. This is not a picnic."

"Then the rain started. I told you Noah was building the Ark on dry ground and this made him appear foolish in the eyes of his neighbors. But after one week of solid downpour you could see the change in the faces of the people who had been hooting at Noah. They began to show an interest in the Ark, and to stand around making little helpful suggestions about the arrangements for the animals, but it was evident to Noah that they were thinking ahead to the possibilities of being squeezed into some dry space fit for humans. Of course they were more concerned for the goats and sheep and camels than they were for rhino and hippo and wildebeest quarters because they thought the world would be just as well off without some of those exotic beasts, but Noah just ignored them and went on with his work. He directed Ham to bring some more hay for the elephants.

"After about two weeks of rain without any letup, some of the neighbors began to hint that they would like to go along and help Noah with things, there being obviously a lot of work involved in caring, for so many animals, but Noah was not having any of their help or their company either. He said "You are not included in God's plan for this boat ride. In fact, you are expressly excluded." And when the waters had risen so that the boat was floating and the neighbors were sitting on their rooftops Noah shut the doors and windows and waved goodbye to them, and though his voice was drowned out by the sound of the waters, he gave his fellowmen a short but pointed sermon: "You are the real reason for it all, so as you go to your reward under the waves, you can claim that you were considered important enough for God to flood the whole earth just to get rid of you and put an end to your wicked ways. Happy drowning." And the Ark sailed.

"Even Mrs. Noah was convinced now that her husband was a man of great sagacity and she joined in the celebration by saying that the women who thought she was not good enough to belong to their social club could swallow enough water to make them think twice, and this remark was not good enough to make it in the Books of Wisdom, but the Ark was floating free and all the landmarks had disappeared, and there was water water everywhere, to use a hackneyed expression, but Noah had anticipated the need for fresh drinking water, and he had stored barrels of it, picking up the empty beer barrels from the nearby grog shops at a bargain, but he could hardly be expected to realize how much water the elephants would want. Mrs. Noah, when they had been out to sea about four days said, the thirsty animals drink so much water I don't have enough for cooking and washing.

"Camels," she said with a snort to match that of a disgruntled camel, "I have been told they can go for days without water but you want them to have it every day whether the boys get a bath or not. And the elephants have got to suck it up and spray their whole bodies with it to cool themselves." It was a real problem which could only get worse as the rain continued to fall and even what they caught in tubs didn't help much because the Ark didn't have decks to set the tubs on. A body had to stand out wherever he could and risk drowning to catch a tub full of water. Noah listened to her complaining until he grew vexed with her and he gave her a short answer: "Tell it to God."

"Well, you can easily imagine that all that togetherness inside a boat reeking with the odors of all those animals put a strain on the marriage of Noah and his wife. But what's a marriage that's never been tested? Nobody really knows whether two people are fitted to one another until they have ridden out a flood. So Noah's Ark sailed and it floated and it cruised all around the world but they didn't see any of the sights that a world cruise normally provides because the whole world was covered with water. And Noah didn't have any navigational skills, but that didn't matter, as Mrs. Noah pointed out to him one evening when she was in a snit over everything being wet and smelly in that stinking boat, and Noah said "You are right for once. It doesn't matter which direction we are going because there is no place to land anywhere anyway. So we just sail on as the Lord wills."

"So you can see by this reply that Noah made to his wife's complaint that he was a man of deep religious conviction. But this did not make Mrs. Noah happy nor even contented. Nevertheless, Noah and the three boys, Shem, Ham and Japheth, were too busy feeding and watering the wild life pushing dung overboard to really do any serious domestic in fighting. But after a long while, even after the rain stopped, they were still just floating on water until one day they felt a crunch underneath the boat and they knew, that the boat had struck something more solid than water. It didn't move so they knew they hadn't run up onto the back of a whale. It had to mean that land or a rock or something solid was close by and Noah turned the dove loose, saying to the bird "You go for it. If you find anything green, bring it back because things are getting pretty close here in the boat. If you don't find any place to put down, keep on looking and try to get back to the boat, but if you don't make it well, just think about the roaring and bellowing and the God awful stink of this boat. That will help."

"The noise was getting on Noah's nerves. The worst of it was the monkey cage. "Crazy monkeys," Noah remarked to his sons. "Swinging back and forth in their cage and chattering away like some of the people we used to know back before the flood. I don't understand why God wanted me to bring a pair of them. They will develop into a whole new race that will be as bad as the one that was drowned. I have a notion to drop them overboard." But at about that time the dove came back with a green sprig in its beak and Noah forgot all about the monkeys, and you can bet that bird got a royal welcome. Noah fed it an extra ten grains of wheat and said some real nice things about it, even prophesying that the dove would figure big in future revelations that God might want to make to the new people who would inhabit the earth now that He had got rid of all the doomed sinners and could start over with him, Noah, who had shown that he knew what God put ears on the sides of a man's head for.

"So the water went down and the boat settled on mount Ararat, wherever that is, and Noah and the boys started unloading all those animals. This took a while because when they stepped out and saw water all around some of them wanted to bolt back inside. But Noah had had enough and he shoved them all out and told them to make the best of what they found. The animals splashed around for a while and they soon got the hang of it and bolted off, exploring the earth that had been cleaned of sinners, and Noah decided it was time to celebrate, so he went on a big drunk, and I guess, you have read what happened when the boys didn't have any work to do, and they went to check on the old man and found him drunk, and the whole thing started over again, with Ham getting the worst of it."

God seemed to feel that He had told me enough and even more than He had told Pat Robertson, but according to the Genesis account Noah lived three hundred and fifty more years after the Flood and nine hundred and fifty years in all. So he was running a close second to Methusalah himself, but it bothered me so I asked God if he would just enlighten me on that subject of people living so long when they didn't even have social security and medicare to take them through all those golden years. And God said "Well, you must realize that Time does not mean to Me what it does to you. I've got all the time in the universe and nine hundred. and fifty years is like an eye blink to me, but I guess it did seem long to Noah, floating out that flood and then when it was all over, finding that all the coffee shops and places of recreation were gone and nothing for him to do but grow grape vines and sit at home evenings with the old woman and talking about the one big event of their lives. So I'll just tell you it must have seemed longer to Noah than three hundred and fifty years or nine hundred and fifty years would be to you in this fast moving age of modern technology."

He didn't seem willing to tell me any more and I thought I had already upstaged Pat Robertson, so I took what I had and went to my typewriter with it because as I grow older - I'm eighty two now, although I have been told I look sixty seven - I tend to forget things unless I hurry and write them down. So this is my story. Anybody want to try to top it?

CHAPTER FOUR

About That Pillar of Salt

I could see that God was just waiting for me to ask Him a question. He was saying Now what will MY Man with the Pen come up with next? I don't mean to imply that He didn't already know, but that He likes for me to open the conversation. So I did.

"That Pillar of Salt," I said. "It's always been a mystery for me. The whole story, in fact. I guess I would be right in saying it's a myth and not a real historical marker like the statue of the Confederate Soldier on the Court House lawn here in town. But that's all the better for me. Myths make the best stories and I am not hampered in my story telling by facts that may raise questions of accuracy."

"Yes, the problems arise when people confuse myth and history when they are reading the Bible."

"Then I will be on safe grounds if I say The Myth about the Pillar of Salt and Lot's Wife and the Cities of Sodom and Gomorrah?"

"Yes. It's all right with me. But you may be in trouble with some of your Baptist brethren."

"Well, myths are built on some actual event and, to get to the inner core of the myths I don't know where else to go. So I've come to You because if You were not in it, then it wouldn't even be a myth."

"Enough about that. Now you want to know about the Pillar of Salt and you've come to the Right One. Just what do you want to know about it?"

"Well, did You really turn Lot's wife into that Pillar of Salt? In other words, is there a real woman inside it? And if so, just how did she get there?"

"It's part of the Abraham story, as you probably already know, and you may already know that Abraham is somewhere between a Mythic Figure and an historical one. But this is Abraham's extended family. Lot. It was Lot who got off over there in those cities of Sodom and Gomorrah, and that brought Abraham onto the scene."

"I get the impression from the Bible story that You were not happy about what was going on in those towns of Sodom and Gomorrah. I guess it must have been like Half Time at the Super Bowl here, or ..."

"Or worse. Yes, much worse. You must see that the people in Sodom and Gomorrah were hung up on Sex. They were the mythical forebears of some of the popular writers today. I know you have got a few pages into some of them, and I commend you for tripping carefully around the subject yourself. But these people in what we will call S&D just could not get down to the real business of living because of their obsession with Sex."

"I guess you are saying they were not doing anything socially redeeming to the town and they were not, making any contribution to the morals of their society because all they thought about was new ways to perform the Sex Act."

"You have a way of making simple things appear more complicated than they were. I just said they were hung up on Sex and I was fed up with them."

"Well, I could see from the sketchy tale about those men You sent to warn them they were doing some far out things and Lot was not standing up to them the way a nephew of Abraham ought to do. Not being the kind of role model they needed.

"In fact, Lot was caving in and offering his own daughters for their experiments and then when the fire fell and Abraham tried to rescue Lot and his family, Lot's wife ..."

"Yes, but don't get ahead of the story. Your eagerness to get to the part about Lot's wife is understandable, but there is something before that."

"I would be happy to know what it is."

"And I am happy to tell you that it was that same old fertility cult that we have talked about in another context. The one My Man Elijah was dealing with. That was at the bottom of it all. They had made Sex the center piece of their religion. Baal was their big whore master. He had set up shrines with both men and women carrying on the Trade. It was sanctified Sex because this was the way they worshipped Baal."

"Outrageous," I exclaimed. "I reckon this really did tick you off. No wonder You set Elijah on those Priests of Baal and ..."

"The story about the Priests of Baal dancing around trying to start a fire, and then Elijah just calling down fire from heaven has certainly caught the imagination of people for hundreds of years, and they do get the idea that I am the real God, and Baal has no power, but most people miss the message that it was necessary to get this matter of Sex clarified and in its proper place in My People's religion."

"And You did it in a very dramatic way and I guess people won't forget it either."

"Well, it's not that I am opposed to Sex. It is the big Christmas Gift to Man. And I even set My seal on My People by requiring them to be circumcised as a sign that the power of sex, of procreation, of continuing Life, was MY Gift to Man, and he must handle it responsibly, even reverently, in the recognition that I had consecrated his organ of procreation of Life to the carrying out of My Purpose for Man."

"Boy. Oh, excuse me for that. But this is real heavy stuff. I reckon most of the Dooms Day preachers up there in the pulpits don't even realize ..."

"Nobody does. Nobody would even dare to guess that I wanted Adam and Eve to discover the Secret of Life in the Garden of Eden. And you just look at what it's all come to now. But what was going on in S & G was unproductive. It was getting people off the track. Something had to be done about it. And I was the One who had to do it. So I did. But I gave them all adequate warning. And I have to say that My Man Abraham did all he could to spare them the ultimate judgment by fire. But Lot's wife. She's the one you want to know about."

"She's the one. And she was not even mentioned until the very end of the story that's told in the Bible. But I don't reckon she was just hiding under the bed all the time that the tension was building up over the corruption of the society in S & G. So naturally she appears to me in the guise of Mystery Woman, the Femme Fatale who was threatening to blow the whole rescue effort to pieces. So she is the one I want to know about. I reckon I know enough about Lot and what happened to his two daughters. But all I'm told about Lot's wife is that she was turned into a pillar of salt and that is the mystery that brought me to You for additional information today."

"Yes. Lot's wife. Well, she was what you might call a Wanton Woman. Or else she had just got city life in her blood, and she was not willing to go back to living in tents out there on the desert with nothing more interesting than goats and camels for company, so when Abraham and Lot tried to evacuate the doomed city, Lot's wife put up a fight and said she wasn't going. The men prevailed, at first, dragging her along, but she couldn't give it up and well, does that explain the Pillar of Salt?"

"Well, not entirely, but I reckon You will always keep some things to Yourself and leave me pondering just to keep me in my place."

"That in itself would be a good thing because as long as you are wondering about things there is the chance that you might learn something useful. It is when the wonder goes out of religion and is replaced by complacency and a belief system that is fixed in a Creed, and you think you know all there is to be known because you have memorized the Creed, now that's when I am tempted to knock down everything and start over"

"Sure. But why Salt? Why not just a rock, a boulder, a piece of stone?"

"Salt has the saving, preserving quality, and it adds a sharp taste to things. Lot's wife now stands as a warning, a testimony, a monument, a remembrance that may save others from a similar doom."

With that it seemed that the interview over the Pillar of Salt was over. At least as far as God was concerned. I guess He thought I had earned my Salt and ought to be willing to let it go at that. But I had one more question. I said "What about that story about Lot and his daughters? That was pretty raunchy. it seems to me. Lot getting drunk and having this incestuous relationship with his own daughters. Was that just thrown in there to add a little spice to it?"

"Nothing is just thrown in with no good reason for it. This was to say that the destruction of Sodom and Gomorrah, and the Pillar of Salt, all was unsuccessful because Man will fall right back into his bad ways, even when he has been given a Second Chance to make good."

This was terribly discouraging to me. Especially since God added a footnote to it: "Now you watch your step. The game is not over until it is over."

CHAPTER FIVE

ABOUT ABRAHAM

God said He was tired of hearing about Pat Robertson and whether he had given him a special hearing on the Presidential election. "Instead," He said, "If you have a question about Abraham, let's have it."

I had not yet mentioned Abraham, but that's God for you. He knows what I'm thinking about asking Him. But I put it in my own words anyway. I said "What I really want to know is What happened out there by the thorn bush when Abraham seemed to he about to do his boy Isaac in, and then that ram ...?"

"To understand about Abraham and Isaac and the Ram, you have to know what went on beforehand," He said, and He waited for me to rearrange my calendar on old Abraham, and ask Him the right question.

"Well," I said. "I know that all three of the major religions that have come out of the Middle East Judaism, Christianity and Islam claim Abraham as their father and founder. But I can't see that he made any outstanding statement of faith. Wrote nothing. Certainly he made no speech to compare with Lincoln's Gettysburg Address, or Martin Luther King's I Have A Dream. And certainly nothing to compare with Jesus' Sermon on the Mount."

"So start at the beginning," God said. "Go back to the time Abraham discovered Me. Or to put it more realistically, I revealed Myself to him. It was up there in that Chaldean City they called Ur. That's when Abraham's troubles really started. Because to discover a new God means that you come into conflict with the people who are satisfied with the old gods they have been worshipping."

I nodded but I did not really see what God was getting at, and He saw that I didn't see it so He gave me an example from my Western trip of a few years ago.

"You know what happened to the Anasazi Indians out there in the West."

"I know they ran for the rock cliffs for some good reason, and I just figured that they had found a new religious idea. So they had to find a safe place to go with their new religion. Then when they were starved out and it wouldn't rain, they went back into the Indian culture of the SouthWest, so I guess they just gave up whatever new religion they had found because it hadn't worked out."

"Now you start there with Abraham, and don't be in too big a rush to the thornbush."

"A new religion then. And Abraham is ... ?"

"Abraham is run out of Chaldea. Told there is not room there for him and his new God. So he gathers up his family, his clan, his servants and followers, his camels and his sheep, and he heads for the Promised Land. Only at that time it is just known to him as New Ground."

"That must have been traumatic for him though. And does Abraham understand what is happening to him? That is to say, does he know what You are going to require of him?"

"Not by a long shot. He thinks I am going to allow the same behavior as the Chaldean gods do. Just look at the pranks he pulled on Sarah and Pharaoh. And he thought that in a pinch I am going to require the same thing the Chaldean gods do to get deliverance from the troubles he has got himself into."

"And that is ... ?"

"Child sacrifice. Oh yes, when things begin to look bleak for him and the tricks no longer work, he will make the ultimate appeal to Me. Child sacrifice. Isn't that what the Anasazi did at the end before they packed up and left?"

"And that's where Isaac comes in? The Child of Laughter. Abraham's only hope, now that Sarah has driven Hagar and Ishmael off."

"You are beginning to see the Light. Abraham thinks that I am going to require that he sacrifice Isaac to me and this will get him off the hook on all his little tricks and save him from utter destruction in this new land that he has come fighting his way to possession, but unsure of his ability to hold it. Without many sons. And he thinks that if he offers me his only son I will give him many sons in return and he can be sure that his seed will inherit this land.

"Now that's it. But I have told you that Abraham had not yet learned what sort of God I am, and so he did not know what I would require from the people who seek My Face and My Favor. You understand that this was several hundred years before Amos and Micah appeared on the scene with a clear cut statement of my requirements."

"Wow. I wonder what Sarah had to say about all of this Sacrificing Isaac."

"Abraham was not in the habit of asking Sarah what she thought, but when she saw him and the boy getting ready for a trip into the desert, she was suspicious and she asked some questions and she gave him her opinion too."

"What did Sarah say? Certainly not. You two have a good day."

"She said "Where do you think you are going off with my boy?" Isn't that what you have discovered is the wifely reaction to some mysterious and secretive action on the part of her man?"

"It is now, but I just figured that back in those days, well, Abraham would be the boss and Sarah would accept his behavior without question."

"Don't believe it. Sarah put up a fight. And Abraham had to tell her a lie about what he was going to do. Just like that old Greek King lied to his wife about what he was going to do with his daughter. Well, you know more about mythology than you do about the Book. But Abraham told Sarah that he and the boy were just going on a little expedition, something like a religious retreat, into the desert to get close to God, that is, to Me, and he did not mention what he was planning to do to Isaac."

"What else did he tell her, for I assume from what You have said that she did not swallow this, hook line and sinker."

"Besides, he told her, the boy needs to know what life is like out there in the desert, away from the comforts and frills of tent life with servants and a sheepskin to sleep on at night."

"Quite a tale, that. But did this satisfy Sarah?"

"It did not. It only whetted her appetite for the knowledge of what Abraham was really planning to do with her son."

"I notice that You keep referring to Isaac as Her son, not their son."

"Yes. Well, you may remember that there was some question about the boy's paternity because of the men I sent to visit Abraham's tent. And besides, the Jews have always recognized the principle that Maternity is known but Paternity is believed."

"That adds to the mystery of what Abraham was doing, it makes me wonder if there was even a double intention in his mind."

"Singlemindedness is a rare virtue. If it is a virtue. But Abraham was going to sacrifice that boy, and he was not simon pure about it either. I know you will see a parallel here to the story of Oedipus with old King Laius exposing him to the elements and the wild beasts on the mountain. King Laius knew that he had entertained a diplomatic mission from Troy or some other place about nine months before the birth of that boy who came to be called Oedipus."

"I can see that that sort of timing might well account for a lack of family resemblance and that would arouse some suspicions."

"Yes, and Abraham thought that if he made a whole new start, cleared the deck of this questionable card named for Sarah's laughter, things might go better for him."

"But he got away from Sarah with the boy and he had all the implements for making a sacrifice, including the sacrificial victim. None other than Isaac, the only legitimate heir to his fortune."

"Of course the boy had some questions. Boys always do have a lot of curiosity and they ask a lot of questions, most of them beginning with the word Why."

"Naturally," I said, not knowing anything else to say. So I just repeated what God had said. "The boy was naturally curious and a bit suspicious too, I guess."

"You are right about the boy being suspicious as well as mystified because his father was not acting like a normal father going to church with his son tagging along. So the boy wanted to know, and Abraham put him off with some trite answer about God will provide. But this did not satisfy the boy. Animal sacrifice was fairly common at that time, but where was the animal? This was what had the boy upset. And you can imagine his anxiety and fear grew by the minute."

"But You pulled it off with the ram caught in the thorn bush, I guess."

"Oh yes, but people have missed the point of this story for at least two thousand years now. Talking about Abraham's great leap of faith. But let me tell you, I pulled Abraham's chestnuts out of the fire for him with that ram because he was going to sacrifice that boy and I was determined to teach him that I DON'T require human sacrifice. I don't require a father to kill his own son in an attempt to gain favor with me. In fact, that is the way for him to LOSE favor with Me.

"It has been a long hard fight to overcome this thing in Man, and part of it is just plain self preservation, offering a substitute for a life of purity and integrity. Like buying immunity from military service. But your question. Yes. Abraham made a discovery there that day."

I was not going to ask that question but it was because I didn't know what to ask. So I said "So Abraham made a great theological discovery and I guess that was the end of child sacrifice."

"The end of child sacrifice in Israel? I wish. But you remember that fellow who thought he was such a great warrior and he promised to sacrifice to me the first one to come out of his house when he returned home, IF I WOULD GIVE HIM A BIG VICTORY. Well, I let him win, and he returned home victorious, and thinking old Rover the hound dog would be the first out to greet him, but old Rover was off chasing rabbits and it was his favorite little girl who saw him and ran out to greet him."

"I read about how his wife made him sleep on the couch for a week, but did that end it? I mean the child sacrifice?"

"It would seem that was enough. But would you believe that the Church came up with a rebirth of it in their interpretation of what happened to My Son Jesus?"

"How is that?"

"Why, the Church has persisted in the belief that I offered up My Son Jesus as a sacrifice for the sins of men who don't deserve My favor. But now I will ask you Would you do that to your son?"

"Not by the beard of the prophet. Surely somebody has got this matter all screwed up, if You will pardon the expression."

"Neither would they. So they think they have a higher moral standard than I have. Effrontery."

"This is getting mighty close to the church pew now. So how ARE we supposed to see what happened there on the cross?"

"It's really rather simple if you remove the element of magic which people insist on keeping because the magic removes their own responsibility."

"I don't understand ..."

"All right. Listen carefully. Jesus confronted the deadly evil in the religious people of his day, and he defied the terrible power of Rome, and together those two powers did him in."

"And it wasn't You?"

"No more so than it was I requiring Abraham to sacrifice Isaac."

"But what about Jesus Himself?"

"Well, He was uncommonly courageous in confronting Evil, and that sort of thing can easily be seen as a martyr complex, but actually it is just the price that a good man will pay for standing up for what is right, against the entrenched forces of evil power in the world. Look at Ghandi standing with uncovered head under the clubs of the British police force. Look at Martin Luther King and his passive resistance to the dogs and the billy clubs. Look at Socrates drinking off the cup of hemlock rather than compromise on Truth. Do you think I was demanding the blood of these men as my price for letting the rascals off?"

I was astounded now at what I was learning. Why, the whole doctrine of the Church was being challenged by God Himself. "Wow. This is really Big Stuff."

"That's a nontheological way of putting it. But yes, that is just the way it is. Now don't think though that you are going to be invited to preach it in the pulpit of the First Baptist Church next Sunday morning."

"No, Lord. Not unless I want to become a human sacrifice. But just in case I get carried away with this new knowledge and can't resist the temptation to share it with the brethren, do you think you might have a ram, or at least a goat hanging by his horns in a thorn bush nearby?"

"Hah. For a chicken hearted fellow like you? The rams and the goats are safe."

CHAPTER SIX

About Jacob

"Now Lord," I said, pushing my luck because I was challenging some of the Lord's favorite Old Testament characters. But I persisted. "About Jacob. I can't understand why the Jews, Your People as You call them, take such pride in their ancestry by saying they are descended from Abraham, Isaac and Jacob. They even call You the God of Abraham, Isaac and Jacob. As if that is a compliment to You. We have discussed Abraham, and I can see that he had some merits that might balance off his faults. We didn't talk about Isaac because about all I can see that he did was clean out the wells Abraham had dug. That story about his part in getting Rebeccah to marry him is a no winner. His father sends a servant to do the wooing for him and puts her to the test of drawing water for his camels What a romance. Then in his old age and blindness he is gulled by Jacob."

God stopped me at this point and said "That is a very long introduction to a question about Jacob. Do you want to talk about Abraham Isaac and Jacob the way My People repeat that litany of their ancestry? Or do you want to ask Me about Jacob?"

"I'm sorry, Lord, I guess I ought to repent in sackcloth and ashes, but I don't have the proper equipment. But it is Jacob I'm wanting to talk about with You because I figure You are the only One Who can tell me the straight story on him. That's because You wrestled with him, so You were close enough to know."

"Yes, and that wrestling match is critical to an understanding of Jacob, and of course that is what you want to know about if it was really Me Who wrestled with Jacob."

One thing I have learned for sure from these conversations with God is that He is always a jump ahead of me. "Yes, Lord," I said. "This angel business still has me confused. I just can't figure it out."

"Then it's back to the Garden of Eden and the tree of the Knowledge of Good and Evil for you. I have been telling you about the nature of Man. But you are a slow learner, so I will tell you again. The angel is the good part and the demon is the bad part. I hope that makes it simple enough for you. There is more to it but for right now ... Well, the angel wrestling with Jacob is the good part struggling with him to make a decent and honest and brave man of him. Now do I have to tell you about the role of the demon?"

"I reckon the demon must have been in control when he stole his brother's birth right and gulled his old blind father who wasn't smart enough to tell the difference between the hair on a man's hands and a goat skin. And then turned coward when he saw his brother coming toward him out there in the open and thought Esau was out for blood revenge because guilt was eating him."

"You are learning. I never require that My Man know everything. I do require that he be willing to learn something. Now about Jacob's angels."

"Well, people here call it Jacob's Ladder. And the angels are running up and down it between heaven and earth. What's really going on here with the ladder?"

"Jacob is going on. He is a very ambitious boy. comparable to Joseph at this point. That Ladder is something I set up for him to give him an idea of what his goal is. He's not as smart as he ought to be at this point. And his guilt is working pretty hard on him too."

"And the angels? Who are they? Running up and down the ladder."

"The good ones. They are Jacob's potential to join and complete that trinity, ABRAHAM, ISAAC AND JACOB. Nobody ever says Abraham, Isaac and Esau. Yes, he had his hand on Esau's heel at birth. And he kept it there till he got what he wanted. But you see that ladder. Part of the angels are on the down rungs."

"He was a scoundrel. But I guess he about met his match in old Laban, his father-in-law. That was a cheating match. Never watched one that good nor one that gave me more pleasure than that one did."

"I rather enjoyed it Myself."

"Well, explain to me about how Jacob cheated his father-in-law out of his sheep and goats. I don't believe that story about setting up rods at the watering trough."

"Elementary, Dear Supplicant. Genetics. Selective breeding. They do things like that all the time at the agricultural station here. I am surprised that you didn't catch on. With your farm background too."

"Old Laban didn't catch on until he found himself fleeced and skinned by Jacob. I reckon Jacob thought it was a way to get even with old Laban though about Leah and Rachel. Imagine having a trick like that played on the callow youth."

"And Jacob's own behavior to ward Leah and Rachel was, well ... human. I guess it would not meet your President's approval."

"No, and shacking up with the servant girls doesn't meet even my approval. I reckon for some reason known only to the numerologists Jacob had to get twelve sons, and it was a job too big for just two wives."

"You could say that. In fact, you just did. But it's not all that important to the overall plan for My People. And the wrestling match was yet to come."

"That's what really interests me. Would You explain it to me?"

"Yes, the whole thing is about Jacob's contest with Esau. Cheating him and then running away out of fear. And then assailed by guilt. Yes, even Jacob felt guilt. He just never came right out and confessed it. Always tried to cover it over with another attempt to beat the odds at the game table. But the wrestling match. Yes. You could say Jacob was wrestling with Me. Trying to force Me to his will. Well, he won out, in one sense of the word. He won his place in that trinity that you seem to think is not so important. But there it is: Abraham, Isaac, Jacob."

"Wow." I don't know why I have started saying Wow. But the things God says to me when He is talking about His Old Testament Favorites just pulls it out of me. "And You let him prevail?"

"But I touched him where he would feel it, and every step he would take after that he would feel it and know that I had touched him."

"So which Angel were You in that wrestling notch?"

"Both. Yes. I guess you would have to say Both. Because I represented both his higher nature and his lower nature. This was the turning point for Jacob."

"Turning point?"

"Yes, he had to make his peace with his brother Esau who turned out to be a real Big Brother. Esau was not a bad man; he just was not as bright, or as crooked, as Jacob."

When the interview was over, that is, when I thought it was over, I remembered that I had not even brought up my question about the Egypt trip. But I had learned enough to realize that there are now TWO whom I can't figure out: God AND Jacob.

So I came back and said "We didn't talk about Jacob in Egypt."

God seemed amused by this and He said "That's the Joseph Story. We will save that for another time."

CHAPTER SEVEN

About Joseph

God had the last word when we were discussing Jacob, and I didn't think anything about that; He always does. But when He opened up with the first word on Joseph, not even waiting for me to ask a question, I thought it strange, until it dawned on me that the story of Jacob had not ended because he was still involved in the misfortunes of Joseph. In fact, God just came right out and said: "Jacob was responsible for it."

That seemed strange to me too until I went back and read the story in the Book. Then I realized that Jacob had created the feelings of envy and jealousy in Joseph's brothers by showing favoritism for Joseph. That Coat of Many Colors had become a Battle Flag. But God said "It was the dreams."

I said "I always thought dreams of greatness are just part of a boy's growing up."

But God said "all boys do it, but some boys are smart enough to keep it secret from their brothers. Joseph was not."

So, I now began to get the picture. Joseph was dreaming of a greatness that threatened his brothers, and even his father and mother. "And that's what got him thrown into the pit," God said. "And sold into slavery."

"Ishmaelites," I reflected. "Seems to me this thing goes all the way back to Abraham. He allowed his son Ishmael to be banished from the tent by Sarah. And now that I think about it, I keep hearing the same story of fraternal conflict over and over again. Cain and Abel. Isaac and Ishmael. Jacob and Esau. And now it's ten brothers against one. The unfavored ten against Joseph, the son of his darling mother Rachel."

"You have been watching the news about Israel and the Palestinians, I hope."

I had. "No way to miss it," I said. "But ten against one? The odds are against the boy. He doesn't have a chance "

"Not without Me. But then, that's not all the mischief those sons of Jacob caused. That trick about circumcision was very bad. But I have to work with what I have - as witness yourself - and I had to get Joseph down into Egypt some way. I suppose you Baptists would have him volunteer for a foreign mission tour of the Nile when he had things so favorable for him at home."

It was not like God to speak with such irony, but I guess He gets provoked with my obtuseness, and my questions, so I asked another foolish question. "You had to get Joseph into Egypt? Why?"

"Long range plans that you would not understand." Yes, it was obvious that He considered me a slow learner. "But try to see that Egypt was where the power was. Egypt was the center of learning. Egypt was the most advanced civilization of the day. With the possible exception of Athens. Egypt excelled in the arts, in mathematics, in building. Just look at the Pyramids. To use an expression common to your generation: Egypt was where the action was. Egypt had every thing. Except a Joseph."

"But why did Egypt need a Joseph if Egypt had it all?" I was puzzled by this turn of reasoning on God's part.

"Egypt needs a dreamer. A dreamer who could also interpret dreams. And when the Pharaoh started having disturbing dreams, and nobody could tell him what his dreams meant, there was Joseph. I had him in place."

"Yes. A heckuva place. Prison. But why did You set up Joseph to interpret the Pharaoh's dreams?"

"Pharaoh's dreams meant that trouble was on the way. For Egypt and for Jacob now renamed Israel, for he had become a Prince with Me. But if nobody could take those dreams of Pharaoh, and rap out a way of salvation, then a lot of people, Egyptians and Israelites as well, were going to get very hungry. In fact, they were going to die of starvation. You have never seen starvation at first hand. I have."

I wanted to stop talking about starvation. I said "I reckon Joseph's dreams had got him into trouble. Now his ability to interpret dreams was going to get him out of trouble."

"Out of trouble and into Power and Responsibility. Power and Responsibility together made him Egypt's Savior. And Israel's that is to say, Jacob's as well. This is where dreams fit into My Dream for the future."

"Your Dream?"

"Yes. The Dream which you my call Abraham, Isaac and Jacob. But My Dream embraced the whole world. You should have been able to see this when I told you about Jonah. It may be too early to even ask if you saw it and understood it when My son Jesus appeared on the scene, but I keep trying with you, although you do try My Patience at times. It is your good fortune that I have patience."

"I am beginning to get Your Drift now. But what's the necessity of it all? Why do Jacob and his crowd have to go down to Egypt and fall into slavery just like Joseph had done? And then have to fight their way out of it? And endure the hardships of the desert? And then have to fight their way into the Promised Land, or Canaan, whichever You call it? They were there. Abraham, Isaac and Jacob had taken it by hook and crook. Why not just leave them there? They'd be way ahead of the hounds."

"It would have been too easy for them. Men cannot appreciate Freedom unless they have known slavery."

"You mean ...?"

"I mean they would have gone on doing the things they were doing in the days of Noah and the builders of that stupid Tower, and the cities of Sodom and Gomorrah, and they would never have seen themselves as the Redeemed People with a Redemptive Mission to the world. In short, they would never have been ready for My Son."

"Gee Whizz," I said. "I never thought about it that way. I reckon we Americans could never have known the meaning of freedom except for the British. Gee Whizz."

"You may well say Gee Whizz. You so called Christians are good at coming up with euphemisms to take the place of the real words, in the language I gave you. But if you are beginning to see the Light, I am pleased and it will ease your pain as you witness the Hebrew slaves under the whips of the Egyptian task masters."

After God said that to me I was tempted to say "Jesus Christ" the way I had heard others express their amazement at something. But I could not quite bring myself to say it because of the way I had been taught to reverence the name of the Savior, but I did say "Great God" and I felt that He and I had achieved a degree of understanding that would bear it when I was expressing amazement at His Greatness. Besides, I had not actually spoken that Holy Name of Yahweh in a vain or empty or meaningless manner.

"But about these dreams, Lord. I just went back and reread that part of the story, and it seems to me that they are quite transparent. The ones he told at home were readily seen through by his brothers. Now these that the butler and the baker had in prison seem to me to be just as easy to see through."

"Especially AFTER you have read the whole story. But the point is that Joseph can see the meaning when others can't, and that is what brings him to Pharaoh's attention."

"Yes Lord, and Pharaoh's dream is more important than the dreams of the butler and the baker, because Pharaoh is King of Egypt."

"You are right. It is not that I value the life of the King more than the life of the baker. But it is that decisions made by Pharaoh have their effect on all of Egypt, and as it turns out, for people beyond Egypt, and particularly the family of Joseph back up there in Canaan, while the head of the baker rests only on his own neck and bears no such great burden for the world."

"Well now Pharaoh's dream. Joseph easily interpreted it, and since the Egyptians were far more advanced than the Canaanites, and certainly they had hundreds of years of experience to base weather predictions on, isn't it just reasonable to surmise that Pharaoh's Dream is as transparent as the dreams of the butler and the baker?"

"Yes, it is. But I have never been the enemy of Reason. Didn't I give Reason to Man for his benefit? Now you just try to reason it out that Pharaoh himself was not a dumb cluck, and he was always looking for new talent, and he found that new talent in Joseph. Then you will see that the point is that Joseph knew not only the meaning of the dream, but what to do about it. So Pharaoh saw that he had found a smart man, and he put Joseph in charge of the program. Joseph carried it out with a high degree of competency, and as a result, he became My Man for saving both Egypt and Israel from starvation."

"I know. You told me that. I reckon I have just been a dumb ass to keep raising the question."

"Well, imitate Balaam's Ass and you won't be a dumb ass forever. Now, what I want you to see is that Joseph was a very important, even THE vital cog, in My Plan to redeem and deliver My People from Egypt."

"Now Lord, I can't improve on the drama of Joseph and his brothers. I only wish I could equal it for pathos, and that my own tears might soften the blows to the conscience of those ten men; and the feelings of Joseph himself when he saw them are described so well that even the Greek tragic play writers would have to bow to this unknown writer. I could not even touch the soul of Jacob himself when the ten, that is the nine, returned and told their father they must now take Benjamin with them when they would return to Egypt for more grain, and to redeem their brother Simeon who was held hostage there. But I have a question about Joseph though."

"I expected it," God said. "For you are never satisfied with what I have told you in My Book."

"True Lord, but I guess I am just not as smart as the one who wrote this story, so I just have to ask You; there is nowhere else to go."

"Then ask. What is it you want to know about Joseph?"

"Why did Joseph put on that act? Was it to vent his own hostility to his brothers? Was it to lay a guilt trip on them? Had he really become so hard hearted in his exercise of his Power?"

God said "It was no act. It was all real. No playing there. Yes, the anger was real, genuine. And the need to have his revenge on them for what they had done to him was the natural expression of a brother mistreated by them. And the tears, they too were coming from a heart aching for his brothers and family, his old father Jacob and his dead mother Rachel, and his younger brother Benjamin. But he was a man invested with the Power of Egypt, the Power of Life and Death, of Mercy and Revenge, and he bore that Power well."

I could see that God had something more to say to me, and I waited for it. "Remember this. Forgiveness does not come easy and cheap.

You Baptists have been guilty of fostering and promoting a cheap forgiveness. It has got you a lot of church members, but it won't stand up in MY Court."

I wanted to go back to talking about Joseph, and I said "if I could be such a man."

But God said "I don't need You to bear and exercise such Power as I gave to Joseph. But I have given you a different Power, the Power of the Pen, more Powerful and more lasting than the Power of the Sword. See that you use it wisely and well. Write, for I have spoken to you, even as I spoke to My Servants of Old. Be faithful to the Word I have given you, and your reward will be to live forever. For the Spoken Word, once it is written down, never dies."

It seemed to me then that God was going away from me, and a thought struck me, so I called out to Him, and I said "But Joseph pulled off that big land deal, and he brought the Egyptians themselves into vassalage to Pharaoh, while his own family he set up in the best part of the country, in Goshen. No wonder the Egyptians came to hate the Jews. I can just see the Egyptian with the whip in hand, laying it on the shoulders of a Hebrew laborer, and saying 'You Jews stole the family farm from us. Now we are all the slaves of Pharaoh.'"

Then God said "Remember the Tree in the Garden. There is both Good and Evil in Man."

CHAPTER EIGHT

ABOUT MOSES

I thought God might be provoked with me for asking about Moses after we had that long discussion about the Scape Goat and Moses' involvement in that, but Moses is such a big figure in the whole story of God's dealings with Man, and there was so much more that I wanted to know, so I came back to Him and said "Now I reckon that story about the baby Moses in the basket among the bull rushes, and Pharaoh's daughter, is about as romantic as anybody could want unless his taste runs to Days of Our Lives. But I have always wondered about some of the tricks Moses pulled off down there in Egypt. Could you ...?"

"It is always better for you, in addressing a question to Me, to say Would You rather than Could You? But go ahead with your question."

"Well, I can see that the young Moses, all full of fire and patriotism for his own people, would take some risks the way he did when the taskmasters were laying the whips on the backs of the Hebrew slaves. And he was smart to get out of the country to avoid a murder rap over it. But after he came back ... Well, I guess I am getting ahead of myself here because he didn't come back until after the affair of the Burning Bush, and that's the big puzzler for me."

"Yes. The Burning Bush was the turning point in Moses' life. If I had not spoken to him in the Burning Bush he might have spent the rest of his days out there running from the Law in Egypt."

"I was wondering ..."

"Keep it up. Wondering will get you somewhere. The Burning Bush is something worth wondering about. Nothing's more wonderful than for a man to be directly confronted by Me and have to stand his ground as best he can, and when you are standing on Holy Ground, it is always best to take off your shoes. You might do well to remember that."

I glanced down at my big feet and my even bigger shoes, and I felt awkward. Then I slipped my shoes off and said "I had to do that at the security check point in the Atlanta airport, and I resented it there, but with You, it's different." Then I stood there barefooted and wondering.

But He said "It's all right now. You understand as much as you ever will about the Burning Bush. What really concerns you is the job assignment I gave Moses there. He tried to make out that he was tongue tied, but once he got started talking, Aaron could hardly ever get a word in edgewise."

"Well, when he got down there in Pharaoh's court, I assume they had dropped the murder charges, or the statute of limitations had run out after forty years. Anyway, when he gets into court, and gets into a contest of strength, and the Serpent comes back into the picture ... I was wondering about that too."

"The Serpent of the Nile, you could say, because the Snake has always been a figure of mystery and power and the secret of life and death among the Egyptians and the Greeks as well. But the significant thing is that Moses' rod became that Symbol and Embodiment of Power because he had met Me at the Burning Bush, and I hadn't only loosed his tongue, but I had put that Rod of Power in his hand."

"I see," I said, but of course I did not see a thing except a profound mystery. Then God went on talking about Moses. "Moses had the commission from Me to liberate My People from the slavery they had fallen into in Egypt. This means I had to break the power of Egypt's ruling caste. I used the instruments at hand. The Nile furnished most of them. And the people themselves; some of them were willing to lend a hand. But if you will remember that I made the Nile and the people of the Nile, then you will understand that I delivered the people of Israel from Egypt."

"Is that where the Death Angel came in?"

"So you want to know about the Death Angel. Well, yes, you may as well know that was a fine figure of speech. Death Angel. A people in slavery develops its own terroristic band to aid the liberation movement. The darkness of night added to the mystery of it, but it was certainly the straw that broke the back of the Pharaoh's camel, to use one of your expressions in a slightly different way. It is more realistic to say it was the blade that cut the last rope holding the Jews in slavery in Egypt. It was a night of terror followed by a day of flight from vengeance. And the Jews barely got out in time to make it to the waters of the Red Sea when the tide was turning for them."

"I reckon old Pharaoh and his people must have been in a rage to get their revenge on those murdering Jews. They must have thrown caution to the winds, or the officer in charge of those charioteers had faulty intelligence about the tides. They plunged in there after the fleeing Hebrews without considering the time of day and got caught by the returning tide."

"You reckon right on that too, and it was a close call for the Jews themselves. A narrow escape. An experience they would never forget. My prophets would never let them forget it either. Not even to this day. They could feel the hot breath of the horses on their necks, and they could see the tide beginning to roll back in and they know what deliverance means. But then they soon forgot Who delivered them, and that explains their complaining to Moses about the food and water shortages out there in the desert."

"I was never able to understand why You took it so personally when Moses struck that Rock and the water just gushed out of it. Seems to me that ..."

"Moses had a hot temper; he was a lot like you in that respect. Only there was a lot more riding on Moses' temper than there is with you. Although I will not diminish the importance of the risk you took with My people out there in Owen County when you sent them all home because they had fallen asleep on your sermon."

"But they had no business staying up all night at the Saturday night barn dance and then coming in there on Sunday morning all bleary eyed and ..."

"Let's just say you were hot headed and Raymond was right about the need for a little more humor and a little less anger in a situation like that. But to get back to Moses ... He would forget at times when he was addressing Me or those Jews he was responsible for. He had to learn that he was responsible to Me for Them. They were My People and so they were a Part of Me, just like those sleepy heads out there at the old Salem Baptist Church were Members of the Body of Christ and you sent them home without a benediction. So yes, Moses got the water, but he got the back of My Hand too because he forgot that I was in charge."

"Well, nobody's perfect, and I guess You knew Your Man when you picked Him. And if Moses hadn't learned Who he was dealing with at the Burning Bush, he certainly learned it on the mountain."

"Right. But you have not asked about the pillar of fire by night and the cloud of smoke by day. So you must have forgotten that, or else you think you already understand."

"I had just forgotten it for the moment, and in my haste to get to the mountain top. But that is important, and I don't think I understand it at all. It seems to me that everything in the Promised Land must have been on fire, and I am surprised that there was anything left for the Jews when they got there."

"And you still won't understand even after I tell you, but that was just to let them know that I was out there leading them and keeping them on track. A pack of slaves brought up on the banks of the Nile would be lost out there in the desert and they would be running around in circles like a dog chasing his own tail. Then with a little more urging from the nincompoops in the crowd. They would have run back to Egypt like a hungry ass seeking his stall at night. That is just what some of them wanted to do every time the going got rough and they had forgotten how the whip feels when the Egyptian taskmasters applied it to their naked shoulders."

"So that was You out there in the Fire and the Smoke. Now can I ask about the forty days on the mountain?"

"I would say that you just did."

"Well, what I mean is: What was Moses doing up there all that while?" I wanted to ask what God was doing up there on the mountain, but I didn't dare. "I read that he came back with those two rocks that he said had the ten commandments written on them. But forty days and forty nights. And that's all?"

"It is obvious that you never did any writing in stone. But you are right in a way. The rock work did not take up that much time. We had to reach an understanding. That is, Moses had to come to an understanding of what I was saying to him."

"Then there was a problem?"

"Moses had a problem."

"What was Moses' problem? If I may ask."

"Actually, Moses was not certain that he could get those people out there to obey the Laws that I was requiring. He did not think they were ready for it, was the way he tried to put it to me. But you should have seen that in what I told you about the Scape Goat and the Day of Atonement."

"I did see it. But did Moses put up a strong objection to any particular one of the Laws?"

"Moses put up a strong objection to putting those people under Laws that he was unable to enforce."

"Well, that seems reasonable to me. Sometimes I wonder about our Congressmen ..."

"Your Congressmen have some problems that even Moses had not dreamed of."

"Then You convinced Moses but it took forty days and nights to do it."

"Forty is just a good round number signifying completion. But in those forty days and nights I made Moses immortal."

"I'll say You did. He is certainly the Big Man in both the religion of the Jews and that of the Christians. I don't know that much about the Muslim, but ..."

"Moses is what I made him, but he deserves all the credit he gets."

"But did he really write the first five books of the Bible the way the Baptists say he did?"

"He wrote enough to insure his place in both history and literature. Those ten words would do that. An excellent example for you to follow too."

"I always wondered about that account of his death there at the end of the fifth book."

"Never you mind about that. Every man writes his own epitaph. You just see to it that something good is said about you when you go. That is, when you come to Me, I mean."

"Like...?"

"Like... he told it the way the Lord gave it to him."

CHAPTER NINE

About That Damn Goat

Moses came down off the mountain with those laws - ten of them - all chiseled in stone, and he laid them on the children of Israel and said "These are not suggestions for your consideration; they are LAWS. Obey them and you are in good standing with God his name is Yahweh and don't forget that but break them, any one of them, and you are in camel dung up to your eyeballs. Now here they are, all ten of them. Laws. Torah.

"But Moses, ten of them?" exclaimed Jasha, the head man in the tribe Reuben. "And you were up on the mountain forty days and forty nights. It seems to me that you could have done better than come back here with TEN LAWS that are going to be hard, maybe impossible for us to enforce on this wild band of desert nomads only recently escaped from slavery in Egypt." Jasha was about to say "What sort of negotiator are you anyway?" But he stopped himself and started to say "Couldn't you ...?"

Even then Moses cut him off. "I tried," Moses said. "In fact, we started with twelve, and I got Him down to ten, And you know how He is about the number twelve. Well, no need to tell you what the other two were. It would only tempt you to break them. But these ten are not negotiable. Yahweh means business, and you will not overlook the fact that the very first one binds you tighter than the saddle girth on your camel. Hear, O Israel, I am Yahweh your God."

A couple of other tribal leaders tried to be heard. Abinidab wanted to point out the difficulty of always telling the truth, and Jedidiah said it is almost impossible not to want another man's wife if she is more attractive than your own. But Moses was adamant. "Written in stone" he said. "Not negotiable," he added.

Abinidab and Jedidiah did not appear to be convinced; Moses said "Try to remember the whips of the Egyptian taskmasters. And remember what happened when we came to the Red Sea with Pharaoh's charioteers hot on our heels. Those whips are like the bite of a fly in comparison to what Yahweh will do to you. And the safe passage through the water is but a foretaste of the good things He has promised. If you obey." While this was soaking in, Moses said "Need I say anymore?"

So all the tribal chieftains pledged their troth to the Ten Commandments and vowed to enforce them on the men and women of their tribes, and to see that the children would have them constantly before them as they were growing up.

All of that sounds good, but it is hard to do. Even before Moses came down from the mountain with the stone tablets, the people had made themselves an idol, a golden calf, in imitation of what they had seen in Egypt, and they were dancing around the golden calf and getting themselves all worked up for some exciting activity with their neighbor's wives. Moses put a stop to this foolishness with some effective treatment. He had the Golden Calf melted down and he made the revelers drink it. No doubt it sat heavy on their stomachs, but it would be a memorable experience often referred to as "the gold treatment." Anti-aphrodisiac. Negative sexual stimulant.

It didn't stop the people from sinning. That is to say, they broke some more of the commandments, and although nobody was found to be in violation of ALL the laws, every one of the laws had been broken by Somebody before they could get their bearings on the Promised

Land and make a workable plan for going in and taking over from the people who already occupied it and had not yet learned that Yahweh, the God of Abraham, Isaac and Jacob, had promised it to these Wandering Jews.

So Moses was forced to do something about what had become an impossible situation. That is to say, he had a sinful people and a God who would not tolerate their sinfulness, and so he came up with THE DAY OF ATONEMENT.

Here is the way The Day of Atonement would work. Once each year, the sinners, those who had broken the Law, which just about covered everybody, would come together and confess their sins. Then their sins would be laid, ceremonially and symbolically, on the head of the Goat who would be known as THE SCAPE GOAT. The Scape Goat would then become a Sacrificial animal to bear away the sins of all these repentant Jews, and Yahweh would accept the Goat as a substitute for all the sinful Jews who had broken the Law given to Moses on the mountain. It turned out, upon reflection on the sinner's part and examination on the part of Moses, that everybody had broken at least one of the Laws and some had broken many of them, Moses decided to make the Scape Goat serve as a sacrifice for the whole kit and kaboodle of sinful Jews. But he required each sinner to come forward and confess his sin as he laid it on the Scape Goat's head.

On that first Day of Atonement the sinners were reluctant to come forward and confess, and the silence was becoming oppressive as well as embarrassing, until Moses spoke very severely to them. "It is no good to stand here like mute stones. Yahweh knows you have sinned; I know you have sinned; you know you have sinned. You may as well come forward and get rid of it."

After Moses said this, looking into the faces of the people with a penetrating gaze, Eleazer ben Sidon came forward with stumbling steps. He stood in front of Moses and said "I have sinned ... I have not honored my father and my mother as I should. They cared for me and met all my needs when I was but a babe and a child, taught me the things I needed to know, admonished me always to do good.

How often have I heard my mother say to me Now you be a good boy. And my father say Act in a manner to make me proud of you. And yet I have neglected them in their old age, and I have not met their needs as the Law requires me to do."

Eleazer ben Sidon did not say what the particulars of the case were. He did not say whether his parents were hungry or their tent leaked, or if there was nobody to herd their goats and sheep. But he had come close enough, and Moses admonished him to lay his hands on the goat's head and transfer this guilt to the goat, "See that you do honor your father and mother from this day forward, lest Yahweh withdraw his protective care from over your own head. Then Eleazer felt a great weight fall from his chest, and he turned back to the embrace of his aged father and mother.

Encouraged by this successful example, Adoniram ben Hadad crept forward and admitted that he had broken the Law of the Sabbath by doing a little work that he thought just would not wait. He had neglected to put out feed for his little flock of sheep on the day before the Sabbath. "Their crying moved me to feed them. I sinned, Moses." And with this confession, Adoniram ben Hadad placed his trembling hands on the goat's head, smiled weakly at Moses, and hid himself in the crowd of people gathered about the goat. Some of them looked at him disapprovingly for having done this labor on the Sabbath, and others felt that he bad done the right thing to feed the hungry lambs.

Next was Jehu ben Jodiah. He was a man highly respected by friends and neighbors and the least suspect of lawlessness. so the people gasped in surprise when he approached Moses, and they held their breath as he confessed that he had stolen a lamb from his neighbor's flock. "They were twins," he explained, "born to the same ewe. My own ewe had brought forth a dead lamb, and in the night I took one of the twins and gave it to my ewe. My neighbor slept and did not know, but I have not slept well since that night. I wish to rid myself of this sin." Then he laid that sin on the goat's head.

Fire did not fall from heaven, the thief did not drop dead. and the wronged neighbor reasoned that he would require the stolen lamb of Jehu ben Jodiah. But before any such action could be taken, Obadiah of the tribe of Levi, pushed through the crowd, knelt before Moses and confessed that in a fit of anger he had taken the name of Yahweh in vain. "I uttered a curse upon my enemy in Yahweh's name. Now, I repent, for my enemy prospers and I am miserable." He laid the guilt onto the goat, turned away, and embraced the man he had cursed.

Then a little man named Elihu from the tribe of Benjamin admitted that he coveted his neighbor's ox. The ox, a big orange spotted animal was strong and healthy whereas Elihu's own ox was a scrawny creature with its hair falling off in spots, and many times as he gazed at the magnificent creature that belonged to his neighbor, Elihu would wish that something would happen so that the man's ox might fall into his possession. He had, in fact, had the same thoughts about his neighbor's wife who was healthy and attractive while his own wife was both ugly and sickly. But he did not confess this about his neighbor's wife, only that he had coveted his neighbor's ox. Now he laid his hands tentatively on the goat's head, as if he thought his secret sin would be revealed, then fled from before Moses' face.

Emboldened by the confession of Elihu, and suspecting that Elihu's covetous eyes had included the woman, Jezreel ben Goram rushed forward to confess his own sin. Rushed lest he lose the courage to make the confession of his sin. The sin was an actual adultery with a woman whose name he would not reveal, nor would he tell the whole truth of the matter. His own wife had died of a disease recently, and so he no longer feared that she would know. But he believed that Yahweh had struck close to him as a warning in the confession by Elihu. Now he wished to be totally absolved of his sin, and he pressed his hands on the goat's head so hard that the goat objected by tossing his head and bleating even as Jezreel ben Goram prayed that he might be forgiven.

Although Moses searched the face and the soul of Jezreel, the man's confession was only a half truth and the worse half was a lie. For he said that the woman had waylaid him and pressed herself upon him and now he had no desire for her but he feared that she would be stoned and her children be left motherless if he revealed her name. This left several of the men who stood nearby wondering if their own wives were the one with whom Jezreel ben Goram had lain, and they vowed to watch him closely whenever he came about their tents.

Jonadab of the tribe of Manassas came forward, trembling and shaking, his eyes cast down and his countenance blanched. He had, he confessed, wrongly accused his neighbor of stealing a sheep, and had made the case so convincingly that the neighbor had been forced by a court of the elders to pay the price of the sheep, but the sheep had in fact died of a disease and Jonadab had buried it and had accused the neighbor of stealing and slaughtering it. Now he wanted to be able to forget about the sheep, and he laid it onto the goat's head and returned to his family, but the man who had been wrongly accused gave him a hard look and purposed to get even with him.

Josiah ben Achbad confessed that he had not loved Yahweh his God as he was required by the Law to do, but he had neglected his prayers and his worship, and had lived his life in a worldly fashion, loving wealth and pleasure more than humility before God. Josiah's neighbors had heard his pious self accusations before, and they took them to be his way of trying to pressure others to be more religious than he himself was willing to be, so they did not take this confession seriously. Indeed, they even scoffed at him and winked at one another when he made his claim to sinfulness. But he touched the head of the goat, ducked his own head to avoid the eyes of the people who stood close by, and disappeared into the crowd. They made way for him but they laughed at him as he passed.

Jesse ben Uriah came forward and said that he had made a graven image and had worshipped it, but it had proved to be powerless, for his flocks still suffered from disease and his camel was mean tempered. He wanted all the Israelites to know that he now gave full allegiance to Yahweh, for he realized that the gods made by men's hands were at best a poor work of art and at worst an abomination. Therefore he abhorred them all and would henceforth worship only the God who had delivered His people from Egypt and had spoken to Moses on the mountain amid fire and terrible things. He placed his hands on the goat's head and said that he now cursed all the gods of the heathen and hoped they would all be burned in a fire, even as he had burned the one he had made and who had proved ineffective.

Nobody confessed to murder. There was one man in the group who had murdered a man though. This was known because a man had been murdered and the crime remained a mystery that disturbed his friends and family. But the murderer did not confess. Nevertheless, because he had done it he suffered day and night because of the fear that his act might become known and he would be stoned to death by his fellows.

Although Moses waited for five minutes in silence, his eyes searching the faces of all the men around him, the murderer did not come forward because of his fear. He kept still and hoped that even the goat would not look in his direction. The goat, loaded down now with the sins of the children of Israel waited to see what would happen to him next. What happened was that they tied a heavy rope about the goat's neck, and two strong young men, one leading and the other following behind, took the goat away into the desert. Neither of the two young men had made a public confession, so it was assumed that they were qualified to escort the sin laden goat into the wilderness.

The two young men found an upright rock too heavy to be moved, and they tied the rope to that rock and turned away to leave the goat there. The goat, seeing that he would be left alone in the desert, a prey to wild animals, to thirst and to hunger, turned pleading eyes upon the two young men, but they ignored his pleas even though he bleated piteously, for they too had their sins which, although unconfessed, remained to give them inner pain in their silence, and they hoped that the goat might carry them away.

So they left the goat crying and looking after them but they did not look back. They returned to the camp and reported the success of their mission. They were praised for it and all Israel retired to the tents, for it had been a long day.

A full moon sailed across the star studded sky while Israel slept. But the morning came and the people were awakened by the frantic and insistent bleating of a goat who stood in the midst of the camp and demanded that his presence be acknowledged with food and water and human kindness and restoration to the herd or flock from which he had been taken to bear away the sins of the people.

When Moses was summoned he came, followed by his brother Aaron, and he found the goat with a chewed and frayed piece of rope hanging about his neck. The goat seemed pleased to see Moses, and when Moses' brother Aaron had drawn his priestly robes tightly about himself, he stood speechless for a moment, then he turned to Moses and said "That damn goat has come back."

Then Moses raised the staff that he carried in his hand, and he struck a large rock that stood in the midst of the camp, and he said "Verily this is a sinful people and the wrath of Yahweh shall fall upon them."

The goat looked up, first into the face of Aaron and then into the face of Moses, and Aaron turned to Moses and said "Now what will we do with the Scape goat?"

CHAPTER TEN

About Joshua and the Walls of Jericho

"Well, I just don't understand it, Lord," I said. I had a visual image of the utter destruction of the city of Jericho, with all those people and animals slain by the sword. The protecting wall lay flat on the ground. "And those rampaging Jews. They just blew a blast on the rams' horns and shouted like the people I hear at a ball game, and the walls came tumbling down. Please explain."

"You have read the story in My Book. What more do you need?"

"Yes, Lord, but what's the meaning of it all? Percussion? Earthquake? Breaking the Sound Barrier? What?"

"You need to go back to the beginning."

"No doubt, Lord. But where is the beginning?"

I thought for a moment we might be going back to the Garden of Eden, since that is where He usually takes me.

"It begins with the two spies."

"The two spies? And the harlot named Rahab?"

"Yes, a good woman, Rahab."

"I have noticed Your preference for these fallen women. Even Your Son Jesus."

"Yes, they are some of the best people I have. Honest. No hiding what they do."

"I don't even understand this part of the story. How will I ever understand the falling walls?"

"I have always been partial to the people at the bottom. They need my help to lift them up. The ones at the top often need to be toppled because of their pride and their greed."

"Agreed. But what were these two spies doing in Jericho? Seems to me they just walked into the lions' den, with Jericho at the top of the hit list. Just what were they doing there?"

"What spies do. They were finding the weakness of Jericho."

"I reckon Jericho was the key city then. If the Hebrews were going to make a successful entrance to the Promised Land they had to take out Jericho ... But after that spectacular crossing of the Jordan River, I guess the people of Jericho must have been a bit edgy."

"Edgy is a mild word for the fear instilled in them by the approach of My People. And when they learned that there were spies in the city, they wanted to hunt them down and kill them before they could get out of town."

"And the harlot. She must have been different from the townspeople. Wonder why the spies went to her house anyway."

"Special, she was the only one in Jericho who could be trusted with the secret."

"Secret? And what was the Secret?"

"I was, of course. And the Ark. But the Ark was a mere symbol of My Presence. When the Ark was with them though, it meant to them, that I was with them. And through Joshua I was telling them how to claim the Promised Land. I wasn't going to just give it to them on a silver platter. They had to fight for it."

"They seem to have been eager for a fight. Especially Joshua."

"Joshua was a worthy successor to Moses. A good man for the job that had to be done. You will remember that he was one of two, Joshua and Caleb, who brought back the encouraging report on that first spying mission."

"Oh yes, the one about the grapes and the grasshoppers. I've always liked that."

"Joshua and Caleb. They were My Men on that mission ... But you wanted to ask Me about the Wall."

"But there must have been some clever psychology involved there. Circling the city that way, with the Ark and the rams' horns, and all in silence, until the seventh day. I guess that must have given the people of Jericho the heebie jeebies."

"With such insight, what do you need from Me?"

"The real answers. Why did the walls fall?"

"Because the will of the people of Jericho fell before the threat of My People for whom even the waters of Jordan opened."

"There's another mystery. The waters of the Jordan just stopping."

"We will come to the waters of the Jordan in due time."

"And another mystery. The Accursed Thing. What in Jericho was the Accursed Thing? It must have been important to rate such a prohibition from You."

"The Accursed Thing? The fallen god of Jericho. My People were always falling back into the attraction for fallen gods. That's why I made the First Commandment First."

"And Joshua told them to avoid the Accursed Thing. I reckon ..."

"You can reckon on, but I am the Lord God and I don't tolerate any rivals. Not even the non gods."

"But some of them disobeyed, and they went for the Accursed Thing as soon as they got inside Jericho."

"And they paid the price of their sin. Yes, they paid."

"That wall still puzzles me though. I am just intrigued by it. This event has even been memorialized in song: Joshua fit the battle of Jericho, and the walls came a tumbling down."

"It was an event worthy of being memorialized in song. Later, you may remember if you have read your New Testament, there was a man on his way to Jericho and he fell among thieves who beat him, stripped him, robbed him and left him for dead."

"Yes, Lord. I guess that's the best known story Jesus ever told. And the most meaningful because it stakes out the new ground of Christianity and its development over the old religion of the Hebrews."

The Lord said "True. It took Me a long time."

"What do you mean? Took YOU a long time?"

"Well, a People and their God are on a journey together. And as they walk together and talk together, they not only come to know one another better; they grow together into a union. They become more alike. Yes. Jesus on the way to Jerusalem is a big advance over Joshua circling the walls of Jericho. Same Name. Joshua/Jesus. Yes. And Me. Same God. But the Word I spoke to you in Jesus is a clearer Word than the Word I spoke through Joshua."

"You mean ...?"

"I mean the God you hear in Jesus' tale of the Jericho Road is a much bigger God than the One in Joshua's tale of tumbling walls and everybody and everything falling under the sword ... But Joshua saved a remnant of Jericho. The harlot and her family. And I have saved a Remnant of My People. The Church. Oh yes, sometimes the Church, My Bride, is a Harlot, but she's still mine. I saved her."

The Lord had started to turn away, and I said "Wait Lord. You wanted me to go back to the beginning. Seems to me the beginning might have been back there when Moses sent spies into the land of Canaan, and all except two of them care back with a wet blanket report. Except Joshua and Caleb. They brought back the grapes and the report the land was flowing with milk and honey."

"That's right. And theirs was the report that was acted on by the Israelites."

"So what happened to the other ten spies who felt like grasshoppers under the feet of giants?"

"With your tender sensitivity about human life, I think you really don't want to know. But I will give you an idea anyway. Grasshoppers get stepped on."

When this had soaked in, I said "Well now Lord, one other thing."

"What now, Little Inquisitor?"

"Well, about the Jordan River. What really happened when the water just stopped coming down? Was there a landslide upstream that blocked it off up there and ..."

"Could be. I created both the water and the dry land. And whenever I want to, I can separate them, and bring them back together."

"Oh, one more question Lord, if You don't mind."

"Yes. What is it?"

"When they were circling the walls of Jericho for seven days with the Ark of the Covenant, and the seven priests going ahead of it with the rams' horns and all, were You in that Box?"

"I am everywhere all the time. Now, you need to be somewhere doing something useful and helpful. Like writing your stories. This one."

CHAPTER ELEVEN

About Old Samuel

"Lord," I said. "This man Samuel. He is a powerful figure in the history of Your People. Occupies a prominent spot in Your Book. But he is hard for me to understand. Even with all the space You gave him in Your Book, I am not sure that I can make sense of him. What sort of man is he, anyway? Please educate me."

The Lord said "You have not overstated the importance of the subject. So we had better start at the beginning instead of so near the end. We will start even before Samuel was born because this was a very unusual accomplishment. One of My best."

"Your best? I suspected You had a Hand in it. But I have a question about that too. You might call it a perplexity."

"What is your question? Why are you perplexed about an event that is taking place every day in My World?"

"Well, You know that we talked about that Fertility Cult back there in Old Testament days. And about what You did at Sodom and Gomorrah to wipe it out, and what Elijah did to the four hundred and fifty priests of the Cult of Baal."

"Don't replay the records we have already listened to. Tell me what's bothering you about Samuel's origin."

"All right. I will just come right out and say it. What did the old priest Eli have to do with the birth of Samuel?"

"It's in the Book and you have read it. Eli gave Hannah a promise and he planted the seed of hope in her barren womb. What more could she ask for? Or you?"

"Yes. Lord. All that. But it is still a mystery to me. Hannah goes up to the shrine at Shiloh because she wants a child and can't get pregnant.. She talks with old Eli the priest who at first thinks she is drunk. But she convinces him that she has this problem. He sends her back home with kind words and in about nine months she has a baby boy. Samuel. What does that name mean anyway? A Gift from God? If so, what is Your role in all this?"

"The birth of a baby is the most wonderful mystery in My World. And the greatest Gift I can bestow on My People. Whenever, wherever, a baby is born I am there. Giving Life with all its Promise, and Hope and the Possibility for Greatness. What more do you need to know about birth?"

"Well, when Hannah took the boy back to Eli at Shiloh, and she gave him to the old priest, what was she saying? He's yours now? I've done my part? Birthed him, suckled him, toilet trained him. Now it's up to you to do your part. Is that it? Is it an admission that Eli is the boy Samuel's father?"

"He belongs to Eli, no matter how you look at it. And he belongs to Me. For Hannah was really giving the boy back to Me. He is the child of promise. My Promise. Of hope. Created by the Word I spoke through Eli My Priest, at Shiloh. Any more questions?"

"Well, I guess not, on that subject anyway. But the boy grew up to become a man . But something happened in the meantime. It was about the Ark. Not the one Noah built. But the real Ark of the Covenant."

"Yes. The Ark. My Ark. The Ark was very important. The Ark said something to My People; something important. What is your question about the Ark?"

"What did the Ark say to Your People? What was the Ark? A Holy Box? God in a Box? Was there something magical about the Ark? Did the Ark have a Power in itself? Was it such a Holy object, like the Holy Grail from which Jesus drank, that it became a visible sign of Your Presence? Were You in the Ark?"

"Now you are thinking about the time the Philistines stole, captured, confiscated the Ark."

"Right. And they thought they had kidnapped You, Yahweh, the God of the Hebrews. They thought they had got hold on the Power that made these people invincible, I guess."

"You are right, so far. They thought they had Me, and this would give them control over My People. Their big mistake was in thinking it would enable them to control Me, use Me for their own purposes, which of course meant to whip those troublesome Jews into submission, and bend them to the yoke of slavery."

"And it backfired on them. Was this Your idea of a big Halloween joke on the Philistines?"

"You could call it that. At any rate, I will not tolerate that sort of behavior even in the people who don't know any better. Ignorance is no excuse. In this case, the Philistines got over their ignorance the painful way. They learned a costly lesson, and they paid in the coin they best understood."

"Pain, I reckon "

"Pain. And a reversal of the whole idea of ransom. They expected the Hebrews to ransom Me. They wound up paying ransom for their own lives to My People to get rid of Me. Or rather the Ark."

"A very neat way of turning the tables on the Philistines. But back there at the shrine. The news that the Ark was taken caused old Eli to fall over backwards and break his neck. And his daughter in law died in giving birth to a child she named Ichabod. I wondered where that name Ichabod came from when I read the story about Ichabod Crane."

"Yes. Ichabod. The glory has departed. But of course her husband was killed in the battle. And she had to demonstrate her grief. Overdid it. Understandable though. Fear, grief, wondering what was to become of her."

"Well, as You say. But the boy Samuel grew up to take the place of the old priest Eli. It was something about Eli's sons being unfit for office."

"Unfit. Euphemism for crookedness. They were abusing My People. I replaced them. Your own leaders ought to take a warning from this."

"Well, it seems that Samuel's own sons turned out badly the same way. I reckon that says something about nepotism."

"It is an office that requires character, and character is not inherited, so the office is not hereditary "

"Then the next thing we get into is kings, and this office is notoriously bad for passing the crown down to despots, idiots and scalawags. Is that why Old Samuel didn't want Your People to have a King? Or maybe I should say Is that why You didn't want them to have a King?"

"Samuel felt pressured into that kingship business. But of course he felt it was a rejection of himself, and saying it was a rejection of Me was a dodge on his part, so he just picked the tallest man in the bunch that showed up. What he didn't realize at the time is that height may be a plus factor for a basket ball player, but it does not make a man any closer to Me. But Samuel picked Saul who looked Kingly."

"Well now, so Samuel was not always acting out Your Mind about things. Does that mean You were not actually behind old Samuel's order to wipe out that little town, men, women, children, sheep, goats and cows? Seems to me that Saul was displaying a more Christian spirit and royal grace than Samuel in this case."

"True. Samuel was a bloodthirsty old Judge. But My Reason for replacing Saul was not that he spared the animals but that he was both paranoid and suicidal, and those characteristics disqualified him for leadership."

"But wasn't it rejection by Samuel and the rise of David to a place of power that caused Saul to be paranoid and suicidal?"

"Not caused. Brought out what was in there.'

"So You replaced Saul with David. And David might have been a man after your own Heart, as it is recorded in the Book, but I suspect he wrote those words himself, or his press agent did. Anyway, it appears to me that David was AFTER Your Heart the way we are given the PURSUIT of happiness in America. It does not mean that the goal or the dream will ever become a reality."

"You are right about that, and I commend you for being able to see the matter in modern perspective. But David had some of the traits of Kingship. Yes, as you would say in your questionable vernacular, David screwed up on that affair with Bathsheba, but you may be overlooking the worst part of that, so I am telling you now in order to get this matter of Kingship straight, when David had Bathsheba's husband who was one of his loyal supporters, killed in battle, he was kicking a leg from under his own throne. That's bad politics as well as immoral. I punished him severely for that. You may remember that it came back to haunt him when his own son Absolam tried to take his throne away from him."

"I guess that the prophet Nathan's judgment on him humiliated him some too."

"Nathan spoke My Judgment on David's action. But later on when he had been sufficiently humbled, I gave him Solomon who was the man best qualified to rule. And without Bathsheba there would have been no Solomon. None of his other sons was fit for the office."

"Yes, Lord. Solomon. Now there was a King with a very good press agent. Wisest man who ever lived. Ha! Isn't that overdoing it a bit? I mean, in addition to Mark Twain's comment on his decision in the child custody case, his attempt to have a thousand wives. Well, three hundred wives and seven hundred concubines, which comes to about the same thing in bed anyway. It would take him three years to get around, allowing for a day of rest once a week. Seems to me that would leave a lot of women frustrated, and a frustrated woman can cause a lot of trouble. I can just imagine him greeting his bedmate on Tuesday night with the question, Now what did you say your name is? and I can hear her saying Don't you remember me? I'm the one who ..."

God said that talking about Solomon was getting a long way from Samuel, but since it might remove the need for another session with me later on, He would just point out to me something I might have overlooked in my eagerness to support the popular American idea about marriage. "A lot of those marriages were matters of inspired political wisdom," He said. "Now David had hewed out a little kingdom there by constant warfare. But the wisdom of Solomon was that he avoided war with all his neighbors by marrying the daughters of the rulers of all the region adjoining him. And who is going to war with Solomon if it means trouble for his favorite little girl?"

I guess I was thinking more about what I would do than about what Solomon should have done, and I said "I still have trouble with the idea of so many wives. I was never able to keep even one woman happy and ..."

But God cut me short at that point and said "You are not Solomon, but if you have some good advice to give on the subject, you might contact your government in Washington and offer it to your President who has the idea that he knows what is good for everybody's marriage bed. I have tried to get through to him but although he claims to be a Born Again Christian, I fear that he was born on the wrong side of the bed."

So I said "I tried to tell him about the War in Iraq, but he ignored my advice and went right ahead and did the wrong thing. I don't reckon he would follow my advice on this matter of same sex marriage, although I think I know more about marriage than he does, having tried it twice; he has only one marriage on his record."

God agreed that if I had only one thirty seven cent stamp I had better affix it in the right hand upper corner of the envelope, in which I enclose payment of my electric bill rather than on one addressed to the President since that might save me from being left in the dark while the one to the President was not apt to get me an invitation to his Prayer Breakfast anyway. So after thinking the matter over, I said "Old Samuel was right about Kings. And if he was alive today, he probably would say the same thing about Presidents."

God always has the Last Word. He said "Presidents, like Kings, are no better than the people they govern. What I suggest for you is that you try to improve your skills at story telling, especially since you are trying to rewrite the stories I have already told in MY Book."

Humility does not come easy for me, but I have to admit that God was right.

CHAPTER TWELVE

About Saul the First King

"Lord," I said, screwing up my courage to approach Him with a question that might be embarrassing. "What about this man Saul, the first King of Israel. Seems to me that he is a tragic figure. Wasn't that a bad way to get the nation off to a start in the world?"

"I would call it a rough transition," God replied. "The nation, My People, had already been formed under Moses, the most powerful you can imagine. And under old Samuel, as you seem inclined to call my last Judge, Israel was strictly a theocracy. Saul had to bear the burden, I might say the punishment, of the transition from a theocracy to a kingdom."

"Old Samuel didn't like the idea of a King. Does this mean that kings are worse than judges?"

"It all depends on character. I have tried to get you to see what the Tree of Knowledge of Good and Evil was for."

"Well then, are You saying that old Samuel just didn't want to relinquish the power that was in his hands? I have always been suspicious of the old bas ... the old judge."

"Samuel knew that he must die, but he didn't want to turn loose the power until he died. He was afraid that a king might think for himself instead of relying on Samuel's judgment, once the king felt the weight of the crown on his head."

"Then I reckon that means Saul was doomed from the beginning because he was not going to hear the same Word from You that old Samuel was hearing."

"Saul was doomed because he would not hear My Word through the mind and the mouth of Samuel."

"But Lord, how could you let it happen that way? Just take that story about the Amalekites. That's blood curdling. Makes me wonder even about You. If Your Son hadn't shed more light on Your character I would still have some questions. Because if old Samuel was getting his message straight from You. My God. What a Story."

"Except for David, I would not have permitted that atrocity."

"Except for David? What do You mean by that?"

"I mean that David was there, waiting to become King. And David was much better qualified for the office than Saul was. But David could become King only by being Saul's son-in-law and the chief warrior in Saul's army."

"Saul's understudy, eh? Standing in the wings, waiting for Saul to goof up and give him his chance at the crown? And from his own father-in-law's head? So what was David learning in this highly dubious role?"

"How not to be king. And at the same time, How to be king ... But the main thing is that David had kingly qualities. He went to the guts of an issue, whether it was a political one, or a military one, or a moral one. And he went for the jugular in a fight. Didn't waste his energies on non-essentials like chasing witches and putting people with familiar spirits out of business. He concentrated on breaking the power of the Philistines. For that was what was standing in the way of Israel becoming a nation to be reckoned with."

"Seems to me that David could be rather sneaky. He went over to the camp of the Philistines and pretended to be with them against Saul. That makes him look like a traitor to his own King and People."

"Yes, David did get inside where he could learn what his enemy was. I remember the Greeks did that at Troy with the wooden horse, but you are a student of mythology and I don't need to go into detail on that."

"But David was just waiting for the crown to be handed to him on the severed head of King Saul."

"True. And he never knew when one of his music therapy sessions with the mad king would end with his own body impaled on a spear."

"Well, I have to admit …"

"You have to admit that I knew what I was doing."

"Yes, Lord, but, well, to change the subject, what about that seance with the witch? I believe she has become known as the Witch of Endor and Shakespeare added a couple more to make one of his stories more interesting. But anyway, that visit to the witch seems to me to be the beginning of the end for Saul."

"It was just the moment before the end. The beginning was the day Samuel set the crown on Saul's head."

"That far back?"

"That far back. Even farther back than that. When Saul was bitten by the Kingship Bug, and decided to enter the Primaries as you would say in America. But his unfitness for office did not come out until he was engaged in battle. Israel required a Leader who was of sound mind as well as a sturdy spear thrower. One who could produce the music that gives life to a nation, not one who has to be tamed from his madness by the music that only his rival could produce for him. One who could interpret the mind of Samuel, and My Own Hope for Israel, not one who clung to Samuel's coat tail and begged him for mercy, and then needed to call up Samuel's ghost to know how the battle, already lost in his own mind, would go on the morrow."

That was a long speech, even for God, and I was not sure I had got it all. I wanted to go back to the seance with the Witch of Endor. I said "Saul seems to have had an obsession with witches. What people here call a thing about them. Samuel noticed that way back there at the time of the battle with AGAG and then ..." I guess my speech was getting a bit long too but God cut me off. "And Saul had outlawed the practice at the very time when he sought out the woman to call Samuel up."

"Right. And when she called up Samuel, she knew that her game was up because she recognized Saul. But I don't understand this business about familiar spirits. I know we went through a terrible ordeal in our own American history when a woman who owned a cat and seemed to be a bit more intelligent than her sisters was in danger of being burned. But this Witch of Endor. Did she really possess occult powers? or did she just know what was on Saul's mind because the King's madness had become common knowledge among the people? After all, if you have a King who is crazy, how can you hide it?"

"No matter how you look at it, the woman saw that the man who stood before her was mad and doomed, as every mad man is doomed. For madness is the doom of one who cannot control the power given to him, but is controlled by that Power. Your own national leaders could very well take a lesson here, but they won't. The people will have to wrest that Power from their hands, and like Samuel transferring the Crown to David's head, give it to a better man, one who will be able to use it for the salvation of the people."

Here was another uncommonly long speech from God, but I could see that He was telling me what I really needed to know from the story of Israel's first and tragic King, Saul. So I waited to see what else He would say to me. I am glad I did. Here it came. "Power is dangerously destructive. It goes to the head and causes men to make bad decisions. Even My Son Jesus was tempted, yes, sorely tempted when he found that He could heal people of their ailments, and feed their hunger, and ... well, walk on water. And the people were hailing Him as the Son of David. But He had good judgment to match the Power. Cost Him His Life. But saved His followers. Those who were true followers and not just hangers on who were hoping for a free ticket to heaven."

I said "I didn't expect all of this when I brought up the subject of Saul and the Witch of Endor."

Then God said "You need to elevate your expectations. There is no telling how much you could learn from listening ... to Me."

I didn't think I could handle any more knowledge than I had already gained and I thought maybe I ought to take a whole new look at my country's problems of leadership, and see if I could apply all that God had told me about Saul.

But then God turned the tables on me. Usually He would want to end the interview before I was done raising questions. This time He was wanting me to raise some more questions. I guess he felt I hadn't learned enough for my own good. He said "Back there when Saul was in his mad fits and David would come and make music to calm his troubled spirits, did it ever occur to you that I might have called you to be a music maker for the troubled spirits of America's leaders? You seem to have got Socrates' idea of being the gadfly on the body politic. Did you ever think of being the balm in Gilead to heal the sinsick and suffering soul?"

I thought that God might have picked the wrong man, and I said "I can't play the piano, and I can't even carry a tune. I'm tone deaf too, I've been told."

"You listen to me, and I will cure your deafness. I'll make you hear the music of the spheres. I'll open your ears to the songs of angels. I'll even enable you to hear the cries of men in their sufferings. If you prove attentive, I will even enable you to hear the still small voice that speaks to the men who walk on the tops of the mountains."

I thought about all that, but I was unable to answer. Except some where inside me I felt the words. "Here am I Lord. Speak."

CHAPTER THIRTEEN

ABOUT SOLOMON

What I wanted to ask God about Solomon was this: How did he manage this marriage to seven hundred women, and then what I see as a quasi marriage to three hundred more known as concubines, and still come off as the wisest man on Earth, when living with one woman had proved to be more than I could handle and I wasn't even a small official in the government here. It seemed to me that Solomon would have been so engrossed in domestic disputes and jealousies, that he never would have had time and energy for affairs of state. And all those building projects would have turned him grey before his time, if my experience of building a house to live in was typical of what a man can get into with building contractors.

But I was afraid God would consider this impertinence on my part if I just opened the discussion with that question, so I decided to ease into the question of Solomon by asking about the conspiracy between the prophet Nathan and Solomon's mother Bathsheba to make old David believe that he had actually decided and announced that he would make Solomon his successor on the throne of Israel. I knew that this could be a touchy subject too, so I said "I am surprised that Nathan, who had humbled David over his behavior with Bathsheba by telling him that story about the little lamb, would now conspire with Bathsheba to get her son Solomon crowned as King. Isn't the old prophet meddling in politics? King making? Help me on this."

Then God said "A Baptist preacher does not have the clout in political circles that My Prophet had in the days of Solomon. That's because you have the Separation of Church and State, at least theoretically, and because you don't have anyone with Nathan's stature. You need to understand that Nathan was the conscience of the Crown. He proved that with David and the Bathsheba incident, and now he was going to confirm it by making Solomon King."

I thought about mentioning Billy Graham. I didn't even consider Pat Robertson but I decided against it because when I thought about Elijah and Samuel, I realized that Baptist preachers today just are not playing in the same league. They are out there saving souls, but men like Samuel and Elijah and Nathan are saving the nation, so I said "I reckon the palace coup was a touchy matter there with old David too far gone to be aroused by Abishag the Shunnamite (she was the pick of the crop in the whole country), and he was not able to remember what he had said about the succession, and could not control his son Adonijah's ambitions.

"Someone had to take the bull by the horns, so to speak," God assured me, and He seemed to be thinking of the altar in the temple, and Joab clinging to the horns of the altar in the hope of being spared his life when Solomon took over the Kingdom. "Adonijah would have worn the crown, except for Nathan."

"Adonijah," I said. "He was older than Solomon. I guess You might say the rightful heir to the throne. But he was passed over for Solomon. Why?"

"YOU might say that Adonijah was the rightful heir. I didn't. Adonijah had more ambition than brains. He tried to take over even before David was dead. No sense of respect. Then he tried to pull off that stupid stunt about Abishag."

"Solomon saw through that like it was made of window glass. And Adonijah's head rolled. What surprises me is that Bathsheba seemed to be in favor of letting Adonijah have Abishag."

"Seemed to be is right. She set him up for the headsman, and he got what he deserved."

"What about that fellow Shemei?"

"You mean his death? Solomon paid him David's debt. He was another stupid one."

"Is it true that David told Solomon to have Joab killed?"

"You found that in My Book, I suppose. Well, either way, Joab was a threat to Solomon. He was David's minister of war, but he tended to forget that he was minister of war and not King. You must see that Joab fitted into David's rule because David was a Man of War. But he didn't fit into Solomon's because Solomon was a Man of Peace."

My mind kept returning to Shemei. I said "Shemei. He was the fellow who turned out to hoot at David during the Absolam Rebellion. And David spared his life but heaped scorn on him by saying 'Don't I know I'm King without killing every dog that barks at me?'" I mentioned this to God and He said "Shemei wasn't smart enough to take a warning. He thought he had got by with it because David spared him, but Solomon saw him for what he was."

"Solomon gave these fellows a second chance, but it was two strikes and you're out."

"Right. A man who makes the same mistake twice does not have much future."

I was beginning to see the wisdom in Solomon's action, but something was still bothering me about it. "You are saying then that Solomon's wisdom was not just a dream."

"I spoke to him in a dream. You need to study dreams. They are the pipeline to the man's mind. Solomon showed he had it already when he asked for the right thing."

"I'll buy the Wisdom Story. But I have some real reservations about that story of the harlots with the baby. Was Solomon really going to cut that baby in two?"

"Solomon set that up, knowing what would happen. It took courage. But courage without wisdom is foolhardiness. He just had more confidence in his own good judgment than you give him credit for. Now that I think about it, a bit more courage on your part in dealing with the moral issues facing the country and the race today would be a plus factor."

"I'll concede that it worked ... for Solomon. Maybe sometime I'll dream and if I do, I'll ask for courage."

"You do that, and I'll give you the wisdom needed to keep your courage in constructive areas."

"Thanks Lord, but before You give me Wisdom I am going to ask a foolish question. Did Solomon really have a thousand wives? And was he able to keep them all happy? Seems to me he might have had some favorites among them and then some good women would get left out in the cold through no malice on Solomon's part but just the sheer numbers."

God answered both of my questions with one word: "Understandably."

When it became evident to me that He was not going to say anything more, I said "Was that wise?"

Then God explained it to me and it became quite clear and simple and easy to understand. "Solomon was a Man of Peace. His father, David, had created the Kingdom with War, and he had wife trouble from the very start. You remember that he married Saul's daughter Michal and that turned out badly. But Solomon expanded the Kingdom by marrying the daughters of all his potential enemies. He never had domestic troubles because he did the things necessary to make those women happy. He built separate houses for them. And he didn't have foreign troubles because he had the daughters of all those foreign powers in his own house."

"Sounds like the ideal setup, but did it really work that well? Or have we been given a picture of a rose covered cottage in which peace and tranquility reside?"

"Well, trouble arose. You should know that if you read My Book; the trouble came from all these foreign women bringing their own gods along and setting them up in their houses. Household gods, you might call them. But I did not like it. I have told you before that I don't tolerate rivals. So yes, Solomon let those women do some things I did not approve, and he spent a lot of money on them, building separate living quarters, and so he had to raise taxes for all the building projects to house all those women."

"Building one house just about broke my back."

"I never said I approved everything Solomon did. But he did it better than anybody else could have done it. And he built the Temple for Me. And he made a contribution to the arts. And he said a lot of wise things. And he became the oracle to speak for me out of the darkness of the Holy of Holies." God seemed to be on a roll about the accomplishments of Solomon, and I felt insignificant by comparison. I certainly did not want to make matters worse by interrupting. He went on: "If you are planning to put your President up against Solomon for the title of Wisest Man, I am withdrawing My Promise to make you wise and brave. In fact, I am putting you in the class with Adonijah and Shemei."

"Not me, Lord. I don't claim to be either wise or brave. But as my Papa said about the Sheriff back home in Georgia, I ain't no plumb damn fool."

"Good Man. I trust you listened to your Papa. I heard him myself when he told you to do as he told you, and not as he did. Good advice, in the light of his performance." Now God had got me thinking about my Papa and that made me sort of uncomfortable. I wanted to go back to talking about Solomon.

So I said "Did Solomon write all those wise Proverbs?" For it seemed to me that Solomon might have collected them and had some court scribe to put them together because he would not have time to sit around thinking up all those wise sayings with a thousand wives on his hands and all the work of building and ruling over a cantankerous people. "Did he?" I insisted.

"Can you think of someone else qualified to speak for the Wisest Man of All Times?" I couldn't, but I had another question, and I was afraid He was going to dismiss me before I could ask it.

"About that one called The Song of Solomon. I reckon it borders on the indelicate to say the least and some of my Baptist Brethren have tried to spiritualize it to make it acceptable for reading in Church. What do You say about it?"

"I say a man with a thousand wives has something more on his mind than building projects and cutting off the heads of little men who are conspiring to steal his crown."

I would have said Amen to that but I have learned that God always has the last word.

CHAPTER FOURTEEN

About Amos and Micah Too

"Now Lord," I said, scratching my chin in perplexity, "What about Your Man Amos? Who is he anyway? He seems to be a most unusual character. He says he is neither a prophet nor the son of a prophet, but if he is not a prophet I don't know what a prophet is."

Then the Lord answered and said "There must be something wrong with you. Don't you even recognize your own kinfolks?"

And for the first time since these conversations with God started, I felt that He might be playing with me. Putting me on is the term people use for this sort of thing. And I said "No Lord. I guess I have missed something important here. I have read what Amos said: and I got some idea of what happened back there. Alot of bad luck for a lot of people. But kinfolks? He just seems like a strange one to me."

God said "You are told in the Book that Amos was a herdsman."

"Yes, Lord. Amos the herdsman from Tekoa. And I reckon Tekoa must be a little town hidden away in the hills. But how does he come off so literate? Is Tekoa a little university town? And how can I claim him as Cousin Amos?"

"Didn't I call you from the dairy? Didn't My Son call Himself a Shepherd. The Good Shepherd, in fact. Is there some reason a man from the hills, and herding goats and sheep can't learn from Me if he keeps his eyes and ears open? Is all the learning limited to the temple and the university? Are you going to tell Me that what little you know was picked up at church and college? What becomes of the native intelligence I gave you?"

"Now that You put it that way, Lord, it seems to me that what they taught me in church was a lot of myths which they said was the truth, and then in college they told me the myths were not true and I ought to stick to the facts which couldn't be proved to be true, and in the final analysis I was thrown back on You and that's why I keep asking You all these questions."

"So where do you get the truth of the matter?"

"From you Lord, but I remember that my Bible teacher in college told me that if I depended on You for the words to speak You would fill my mouth with hot air and gnats."

"Well now, don't be too hard on the Bible professor. He might have been speaking out of his own experience when he just opened his mouth without opening his eyes and his ears."

"Amos then, Lord. Do You mean to tell me he got it all right from You while he was watching over the goats and the sheep? And then he came down to town and told all those city dudes what they never guessed was going to happen to them?"

"That's about it. Except for his having kept his ears open to the news of what was happening all over the country, and his eyes open to the way I work with human events. And of course they were a bit shocked to hear that some bad things were going to happen to them. Things they had not guessed at before."

"And I reckon they didn't jump for joy when they heard it from Amos, and they didn't offer to call him as the pastor of the First Baptist Church of Israel."

"No. Instead they suggested that he apply at the Memorial Baptist Church of Judah. And that failing, he could hold a brush arbor meeting in Samaria."

"Well, just what was it that made Amos so unpopular? I thought people liked to hear a little fire and brimstone from the pulpit."

"A little, yes, but when Amos began to direct the fire at their houses - he called them palaces - they began to feel the heat and they didn't like it."

"But he kept mentioning Your Name. I thought people liked to hear a preacher talk about God. I believe I have heard one little book in the Bible roundly criticized because there is no mention of you in it and folks don't understand how it ever got into the Bible."

"But Amos lit the fire under them when he told them they had underestimated Me."

"Underestimated You? How? Where had they gone wrong on that?"

"Where most people go wrong. They expect Me to ladle out good things for them whether they live right or not. They were living like a pack of godless rascals and Amos told them they were going to ... catch hell from Me for it."

"He seems to me to have a big hang up about those people living in palaces. And he wanted them all to go up in flames. Sounds like a pyromaniac."

"A man who lives in a tent of goat hides pitched out on the mountain will just naturally have some strong negative feelings toward the people living in town houses. No air conditioning back then, but enough luxury to load Amos' guns."

"Gee Whizz God. No wonder they sent him packing back to the hills."

"They did. And when he was only half way through his sermon."

"What? Do you mean there was more? It seems to me that ..."

"Much more. In. fact he only got through the part about what I was going. to do TO them."

"You mean ...?"

"Oh yes, they cut him off before he could tell them what I was going to do FOR them."

"Well, it looked like a complete sermon when I read it."

"Well, he added some to it when he went back up into the hills and settled in with his herd of goats. If you will remember, that is about what I did with you."

"Goats, was it? Well, I have always been partial to goats. My first book of tales."

"If you will listen more closely to Me, I will give you something more important than those goat tales you are so fond of telling. I may even change your pen name to Amos for the A. you have in the middle of it."

"Now Lord, the more I look at what Amos said to those people, the more surprised I am that he ever lived to write it down. I remember the time I wrote that little letter to the editor of the Atlanta Journal and the folks hanged me. It was in effigy, but I believe that if I had said the things to them that Amos said to the people of Israel, it would have been for real. Makes my neck tingle just to think about it."

"A little more and they would have. If you had not had a good wife to curb you a bit ... well, but Amos, the people deserved just what he gave them. This was the beginning of the realization in Israel that I expected a level of BEHAVIOR better than what they were doing. And that if they did not come across with it they would suffer for it."

"But Lord, I've been over what Amos said and I don't see anything but DOOM, unrelieved doom. Honestly, I'm surprised they didn't take his head off."

"You don't see it all? There is one little word of hope … at the end, yes, but there you will find the promise of a remnant, a little seed corn, so to speak, enough to start over."

"Well, thank You God….for nothing."

"Not nothing."

"Not nothing?"

"Like I said, a remnant. Seed corn. I will bring them back, Chastened. When they have learned their lesson. Then I will restore them and they will rebuild. Replant. Eat and drink in the land which I have given them."

"But where are they to learn from all of this?"

"Micah will tell them."

"Micah? What will Micah tell them?"

"Micah will tell them what I require of them."

"And what is that?"

"Read it."

I did, and here is what I found: "What does the Lord require of you, but to do justly, and to love mercy, and to walk humbly with your God."

I said "I think I have got it now Lord. But it is a big assignment when You look at it closely."

"Then do it," He said. "Remember It's the doing that counts."

CHAPTER FIFTEEN

ABOUT BALAAM'S ASS

"Lord," I said, scratching my balding head, and puzzling over what I had just read, "How did this story of Balaam's Ass ever get into Your Book? It's the strangest one I have run across anywhere, and here it is right in the Book of Numbers, which Moses is reputed to have written. At least my Baptist brethren say he did."

"You could well ask that same question about some other things in there that are not as unbelievable as a donkey talking."

"I reckon that's right. I was reading some of the things the venerated Paul was saying about the resurrection, and it staggered my imagination so much that I was tempted to go out to the barn and hold a conversation with the mule. As a matter of fact, I did have a little chat with Taffy and Max."

Taffy, Dear Reader, is my little white Spitz who has lived with me for the past fifteen years. And we talk to one another. That is to say, we communicate well enough for me to know when she wants out and when she wants back inside, and when she is hungry and when she just wants my attention. I guess that's about enough to keep me on my toes; I just never tried to discuss theology with her.

Max is a yellow Manx cat. He has no tail, but that does not mean he does not have a tale to tell. I also say endearing things to him at times, and I have said some harsh things to him when he sank his claws into me. Max talks to me by rubbing against my ankle to tell me that I belong to him and I had better not take up with any stray cats that may come wandering in. He also tells me that he belongs to me by leaping onto my knees where he curls up and sleeps the sleep of the innocent and the secure. There are other messages from time to time, but those two are the most important ones and easiest for me to understand.

And because I grew up on a farm in the days before tractors became the machinery of both choice and necessity, I talked with the mules and horses. "Come up" I would say when I wanted to go. And "Whoa" when I wanted to stop. To go to the right I would sing out "Gee" and when I'd need to veer a bit to the left I would croon "Haw". And I must admit, since honesty is a quality of great value, that on occasions of stress and aggravation I used some language designed to let the mule know what I thought of the mule's character and ancestry. And the mule sometimes spoke to me with teeth and hooves, and with a swishing tail, just to let me know that my performance was not up to the level of acceptability.

But never in my life have I held a conversation with a mule that was anything like the one that went on between Balaam and his she ass. I am not speaking here of the specific content of the conversation either. That will become evident when I come to tell you about the Light that God shed upon this story. And just to set the record straight at the beginning, this story is a Fable. When an animal talks like a man, thinks like a man, and acts like a man, it is a Fable. And it does not matter whether what the animal is saying is wise or foolish. If he is portrayed in anthropomorphic terms, it is a Fable. Not a Myth, or a Fairy Tale. It is a Fable. And this one is one of two Fables that have shown up in my reading of the Book. The other one was a gathering of trees intent upon some such foolishness as choosing a king to rule over them. But this one about Balaam's Ass just takes the cake because it is immediately obvious to the perceptive reader that the Ass is smarter than Balaam, at the beginning of the story. Now that one back there in the Garden of Eden when the Serpent talked to Eve, that's another one that stands alone, and is both sui generis and monogenes, both terms to let you know I studied both Latin and Greek.

But setting aside the Fable part of the story, I am standing in awe before this man Balaam, who had almost escaped my notice while I was dealing with better known characters like Abraham and Moses. Now that I am looking at Balaam though I hear myself saying "What a Man."

So when I came to the Lord with my question about the ASS that talked and took Balaam to task over his mistreatment when the Ass was really trying to keep Balaam from making a big mistake, God saw right off that my question was about Balaam, and not just about the Ass, and then God said to me "You will do well to observe this man Balaam, for he is one in a million because he is incorruptible."

"It might have taken a talking ass to bring him to incorruptibility, but he is surely a man I can admire."

Then the Lord said to me "Go and do likewise," which was exactly what I expected to get from Him because He had put me on the spot about the war we are waging in Iraq and Afghanistan and all over the world, for that matter. It is a war against terror and I have become convinced that we can't win it because we are creating the terrorists we are fighting by killing them, and the Lord is saying to me "You need not offer up any prayers to Me about this matter because I will not authorize you to curse these people, but I will have you to bless them because they are the poor and the downtrodden of the Earth. And I have chosen to lift them up. They are willing to give their lives as a testimony against the power that America wields, and I will bless them because they are the voice of the people beaten down by that Great Power. You can let the Baptists sing God Bless America till their throats are dry, but you will not curse the people who are strapping bombs to their bodies to fight for freedom and dignity."

I wanted to say something patriotic, and I said "But Lord, can't I pray for our troops? Can't I say they are doing the right thing to kill the terrorists?"

But He said "You be like Balaam, and know that I have spoken to you. If it is necessary to get down there on your level and speak through the mouth of an ass then remember that such an ass bore the Mother of Jesus on its back to the place where He was to be born, and such an ass bore Him on its back when he entered the city of Jerusalem to proclaim the advent of the Kingdom of God."

I was about to say that I didn't mean any disrespect for the lowly ass, when God took a surprising turn and said "But if it is necessary for me to speak to you through the Angel who stands in the road barring you from going astray, then." So I kept my mouth shut out of pure fear and God went on speaking to me. "So you just wonder on about the lowly she ass who spoke to Balaam and set him on the right path. Listen and heed the message and speak truth to my people. Speak blessing and not a curse."

Then I was about to go somewhere to get away from that terrible Word He was speaking to me, and He called me back and said "Are you sure you know as much about Balaam as you need to know?"

I thought about it and said "I reckon I really don't know anything about Balaam. Who was he? Where was he going when the ass stopped him? And why was he going there? Why was his curse or his blessing so powerful? Where did he get such clout as to be able to control events and the fortunes of nations with a word? No. I guess I don't know the man at all. Would You mind if we just started over from scratch, so to speak, on Baalam?"

Then God said "I have been patient and have spent a lot of time with you. This time I am going to let you guess it out for yourself. Now, you have the right questions. Let's see if you can come up with the right answers."

"Well," I said. "Balaam is not your ordinary fellow. He is somebody who can make things happen. He can pronounce a curse and all hell will break loose on the one he curses. He can bless, and the sunshine of Heaven will smile on the one he blesses. Now that is translating the Word into Power. And obviously he had been sought out, as I have never been, and offered a reward to speak the Word. That old King who wanted Balaam to put a hex on the Israelites wasn't just offering peanuts for his service. He must have been a wizard, and the old king thought he was a wizard for hire. At least until his ass threw him and he saw the angel.

"Yes, that seems to be the turning point, when he saw the angel. And I have a lot of questions about angels."

Then God said "Yes. Angels. A rather mysterious subject. Even Aquinas only muddied the water when he tried to tell about angels. But angels don't appear to everybody. That is to say, just anybody can't see angels. And Balaam had to be thrown off his ass before he could see the angel standing in front of him. But when Balaam was baffled by the words and actions of his ass, and he found himself in a different frame of reference, and looking out on a world he had not experienced before, why behold, there stood the angel. Here he was talking to the ass and threatening to kill her if only he had his sword, and the next Moment he is facing the sword of My Angel, and the whole world appears to him in a different Light."

Well, I had got God to talking again, but then I could not keep my own tongue in my mouth, and I said "So Balaam was about to be used by that old king to break the back of Israel, Your People, and bring all sorts of bad luck on them by pronouncing a curse on them. The old king wasted twenty one bullocks and twenty one rams trying to get Balaam signed on, but he wouldn't sign on the dotted line. I still don't know who he was but he must have been some sort of traveling magician like those fellows down in Egypt who could make snakes appear. He just comes out of nowhere and goes into nowhere, but he cuts a wide swath because he has a reputation for getting results. I'll bet he could find water in the desert and gold in the sand of my back yard. What I can't figure out though is this: Where did he get this kind of power?"

Then God said "I will have to help you out on that because you seem befuddled. Balaam had an ass that was smarter than his head. But when he did get his eyes open so that he could see the angel, My Angel, that is to say MY Messenger, and he got his ears straight on his head so that he could listen and hear what MY Angel, My Messenger, was saying to him, he became a very effective instrument in My Hands for doing good, for blessing My People who were struggling along and doing the best they could in a hostile and alien land. And so you could say that Balaam was My Man of the Hour."

I was still in shock from the story, and all I could think of to say was "Gee, I hope Balaam fed his ass well that evening as reward for a good day's work."

CHAPTER SIXTEEN

ABOUT SAMSON

"Samson." I said. "The long haired Hero."

And God said "Samson was a favorite of Mine. Very special. If he just hadn't let that woman cut his hair; yes, he could have done wonders for his people. Did a lot as it was. Watched over them for twenty years. But could have done better. But then you could …"

I didn't want to talk about me. I said "It appears to me that Sam pulled off some mighty deeds on behalf of Your People. Or was it just piss and vinegar on his part?"

"I have to take a man where I find him and use him as I can. I don't work with perfect materials."

I had not thought about it that way. "I guess I thought You would pick a man because of his qualifications. But evidently that's not necessarily so." I was going to let it go at that, but I decided to push a little. So I said "But it seems to me that You marked him from birth."

"I did. A Nazirite. Do you know what that means?"

"Well, it means no trips to the barbershop. I know that much."

"That's not all. No wine, and he's excluded from the undertaking business, if you want to be colloquial in your language. But the real thing is that he is consecrated to Me. Chosen to do great things in My Name. To deliver My People from the Philistines. And for that job a man needs more than just long hair and sobriety. He needs character. Samson was good clay but there was a flaw in it."

"A real flaw then? We are now in the job of picking a President for our country. And try as they may to cover it up, they are all flawed."

"Yes, Samson was flawed, but I didn't cut him out or pass over him on that account. In fact, for the job I had in mind, that of breaking the power of the Philistines, he was the best qualified man I had available. But yes, he was flawed."

I thought God was going to tell me what the flaw was, but I guess He wanted me to ask. So I said "I reckon I know what his flaw was, but I had rather hear it from You because we don't always see a man the same way. You and I." I thought that would draw Him out and He would be more specific.

"It probably is not what you are thinking. Because you are thinking it was his weakness for women. It was not that. A weakness for women is just built into a man. It was his inability to keep a secret when he got with a woman. He failed to recognize a fact long established, that once you tell your secret to anyone, certainly to a woman, there is no chance of getting it back. It's out."

"Then You are saying that it was not that Samson was attracted to Philistine women, but that he could not keep his own identity pure in the relationship. And he didn't learn a much needed lesson from his First experience of betrayal."

"Right. You have seen into the character of Samson. Now if you could only make the application to yourself, then you would be getting a double blessing out of our conversations."

I wanted to get the talk away from me and back onto the track, something about the fate of the nation of America, so I said "I reckon that is part of our problem today. I have been thinking of the secret of nuclear power, and our attempt to limit it to us and our close friends. And cloning. We seem to be upset because the Vietnamese have learned how to do it. That may be a long way from Samson, but it makes me wonder."

"Yes, well, you just keep on wondering. And try to make some discoveries that will be a blessing to My People. They all have the secret of nuclear power now and nobody can control that. They have the secret of cloning now, and you won't be able to control the direction it will take. You may even pull the house down like Samson, but the inquiring mind of Man will go on inquiring, and the Evil will go on, along with the Good. You didn't read the sequel to the story of Samson, did you?"

It seemed to me that God was telling me a lot I had not even asked about while there was still a lot He didn't tell me, like the connection between Long Hair and physical strength. But I was afraid I would appear foolish in His Eyes if I asked. So I decided to just let the matter rest until He indicated a willingness to tell me more. Then He said "Now your hair is getting a bit shaggy around the ears, but don't let that give you any big ideas about carrying off the gate posts. At your age you will do well to lift a pen to paper."

Which was just what I did. I hastened to write down what I could remember of what He had told me about Samson. I wanted to get it on paper before I lost any of it, but I might have lost some it anyway, so I hope that my Readers will feel free to talk with God about Samson and learn something more than I did.

CHAPTER SEVENTEEN

About Esther the Queen

"What is it now?" God said as I approached with my yellow legal pad in hand. I could read nothing certain in the way He asked me that question, so I went right ahead with my own question. "It's about Esther, the Queen to King Ahasuerus. She must have been some looker. And more than just looks. Smarts. I'd say. Now, I'd like to know …"

"She was," God said. "Oh, no better looking than Vashti the Queen before her. But a lot smarter. And loyal to her people, the Jews."

I said "But the King, ordering Vashti to come out and be shown off … I can't say that I blame her for refusing to be put on display in front of a crowd of drunken revelers in festive mood. And I can't say that I approve of the King's action in demanding it of her. He must have been drunk himself … And disrespectful of the Queen as a person of more worth than just a beautiful body. Most women would not tolerate that sort of treatment today."

"It was not a smart thing for the King to do. But don't look for smarts among the world's rulers. Just ambition and ruthlessness."

"Well, that helps me to understand American politics a little better. But the old King picked a winner in Esther."

"Haven't you learned yet that it's the woman who picks the man? It just appears to be the other way around, but that is part of the woman's doing too."

"Well, whatever, but what a story. And a puzzler too. I wonder… "

God said "One of the few things I fully approve of about you is your wondering. It signifies that you are not hopeless. You can still learn."

Until God said that I was woolgathering, but that brought me back to the question I wanted to ask. "About that kingdom of old Ahasuerus, was it really that big? I mean from India to Ethiopia? Over a hundred and twenty seven provinces. That's a big empire."

"No sense in telling a story unless you can make it bigger than life. And certainly you can't exaggerate man's ambition to rule."

"Well, anyway, there is room here for a whale of a story. Wish I could."

"Study it, and maybe you will become an effective story teller yourself some day. But what was it that you were wondering?"

"I was wondering how the story writer got all the fixings in there so that Esther would be chosen out of all those beauties and then have the power to rule the heart of the King and control the destiny of the Jews in the whole empire."

"That's why I want you to study the story. But don't forget that I am in control of human events. Kings come and Kings go but am King always."

"That's encouraging, but I have noticed that You are not even mentioned in this story. And people notice that. Some have even told me they wonder how the story got into the Bible. What about that?"

"I don't have to be mentioned in order to be there. These people who are afraid I will drop out of the picture because they don't say "under God" in the pledge of allegiance to the flag, or don't post the ten commandments on the school house door are wasting their tears. Don't worry about Me. I am everywhere, all the time. And in control. You just write. And aim higher than Haman's gallows."

"Well, I would have thought You would at least get credit for saving the Jews. After all, they are Your People."

"You just remember: I AM."

I decided it would be safer to talk about Haman's gallows. I have always had an obsession about gallows, since the time I was hanged down there in Georgia. So I said "Now about Haman's gallows And Haman getting hanged on it the way he did, is that what You call retributive justice?"

"You could call it that, since you seem to like to use big words. I just say Haman got what was coming to Haman. But don't you forget, I am in control, even if nobody mentions My Name."

I drew some hope from this interview. If Esther could do all she did, maybe I could write a story. But God had spoken, and I did not dare say anything more.

CHAPTER EIGHTEEN

About Daniel

"Lord," I said. "What really happened with Daniel in the Lions' Den? I might say In The Fiery Furnace. But I guess it would still be the same question. What about Daniel?"

God said He was glad I asked about Daniel because it would give us an opportunity to switch these conversations onto an optimistic level. "These others, Jonah and Noah and Lot, even Abraham, all fell far short of perfection. But Daniel, now there was one who was just good through and through. I can't fault Daniel on any score. And nobody can say he was not tested! . He would measure up to Job on that matter of testing and come out ahead of him. At least, I never heard any complaints from Daniel."

"Seems to me," I said, "that this Daniel, or Belteshazzar, is just too good to be true. He's on a vegetarian diet and he turns up better looking than the ones who eat good red meat full of protein; he tells the King what his dream means when he hasn't even heard what the dream was; and he is advanced from being a captive slave boy to being the King's Prime Minister without even having an election.

"Now I ask You, God, Is this fellow for real Or am I being set up to accept a hero who is a saint and a wizard and a miracle worker who can see into the future all in one person?"

"Just you wait until you see what his jealous enemies have in store for him. You may not be so eager to swap places with him. After all, being an unread writer is not as bad as facing a pride of hungry lions."

"Well now I'm not hankering after an intimate relationship with the Big Cats, and I found South Georgia warm enough in the Summertime. But I am beginning to see that this man's power would just naturally arouse jealousy and plotting. I guess that's what's meant by the Golden Image. I'm just not clear whether the Image is of the god the Babylonians worshiped, or if was an image of Nubuchadnezzar himself "

"Good wondering too. The answer is simple enough though. Nebuchadnezzar has made himself god, and the image is of the deified king. Babylon being what it was and is, you ought not to have too much trouble with the King's next dream."

"I reckon not, after seeing the U.S. soldiers toppling Saddam's statue from its pedestal. Yes, Lord, Now I see that this Babylonian King had high aspirations matching those of the fellows who built that Tower. And Daniel told him it was all coming tumbling down. Only there would be a stump left, and it might sprout something."

"Yes. A humbling experience to match that of Frederick Barbarossa when he had to stand barefoot in the snow at Canossa when he wanted to be Emperor of the Holy Roman Empire. You remember that, I hope. Unless you were asleep in the Church History class."

"I was awake, but in a Baptist Seminary, old Pope Hildebrand didn't get any more credit than Frederick. So there was not much weeping for Frederick's frozen feet nor for the Pope's tarnished episcopal crown."

"At any rate, you have learned how to ask questions. That's good."

"Thank You Lord. Even in my humility I can endure an occasional pat on the head. But the thing that puzzles me about Daniel is this: I always heard that the messenger of bad news was on his way to the head chopping block. But Daniel. He brings bad news to the King, and he gets promoted to a position of power."

"He is certainly different from the common run of messengers in that respect. I know you must be thinking of his interpretation of the King's dreams. And I hope you realize that I set a high value on telling the truth even when the truth is not flattering to the listener."

"Yes, but that first one, with old Nebuchadnezzar eating grass. Imagine that. But at least there was the promise of something better, once he had learned what it was like to be a lowly animal. But the one with Belshazzar and the handwriting on the wall. No hope whatever of redemption. The King is killed. But Daniel is in the third spot of power in Babylon. I guess that's about like being Speaker of the House if the President gets shot in this country."

"First President over the Princes. But this aroused the jealousy and brought on the trouble for Daniel. Of course, all the others wanted the office he held, and they cleverly planned to undo him with the King."

"I caught that, and it was Daniel's devotion to You that was seen by them as the chink in his armor. I reckon that decree that they got up must have been about as hastily done as the U.S. Congress' bill to give the President the power to go to war against Iraq."

"And with about the same result. It was this bit of foolery that resulted in Daniel being thrown to the lions."

"That's the part that really gets me, Lord. Did Daniel just have a way with the Big Cats? or were You trying to tell us something that we have missed here?" I thought about the way I had put the question and decided to turn it around. "What I mean to say is, Have we missed something You were saying to us in this story of Daniel in the Lions' Den?"

"And if I answer, you will want to know if I put out the fire in the furnace. Or are we talking in riddles about something even more important?"

"Yes. That too. I don't understand it. Well, what I am trying to say is this: You didn't do a thing for Jesus on the Cross. And here is Daniel hobnobbing with the Lions, and here are his three friends, Shadrack, Meshack and Abednego, standing in the fiery furnace and it's like they are wearing asbestos suits of armor."

"Oh, then that is what is bothering you. You, who call yourself a writer, and you don't understand figures of speech. I see now that Miss Florrie left something undone when she was teaching you Latin ... and English."

I was staring bleary eyed when God said "Or is it that you just don't understand about My Son Jesus on the Cross. You think it is remarkable that Daniel survived the Lions' Den and his three friends were not consumed by the fire, but you don't see that Jesus was not touched by the Evil on the Cross because the Good in Him was more powerful than the Evil that nailed Him to the Cross. You don't see that Death really had no power over Him because in Him Life was triumphant."

"Then You are saying ..."

"I am saying that you are a slow learner after all and you will have to wade around in the myths and the stories that are at your level because when you try the really deep waters of My dealings with men in this world, you are just out of your depth. So Christ on the Cross will always be a mystery to you. And maybe even Daniel in the Lions' Den, and Shadrack, Meshack and Abednego in the Fiery Furnace. But don't feel too badly about it. Nobody else understands either. And you are ahead by one jump because now you KNOW THAT YOU DON'T KNOW."

After this Word from the Lord I thought I might have undertaken a task too big for me. Rewriting the Bible. Maybe I had better stick to doing folk tales and little stories about the strange and peculiar people I have known. Maybe some dog and cat stories. And Little Chicken Tales. But yes, I really am out of my depth here.

On the other hand, with Him holding my hand, I might even walk on water. Which brings up the question I want to ask Him about Peter on the Lake of Galilee. I'll make a note of that and next time ...

CHAPTER NINETEEN

About Elijah/Elisha

"Who is it now?" God had become accustomed to my inquiries about famous men in the Bible. And he was patient with me, all things considered. So I just kept plugging away at the job. After all, there was no other way to learn more than what was already written in the Book. So when He opened up the way for me, I just said "Elijah."

That was because Elijah seemed bigger than life, and he cropped up even in the life of Jesus. So I said "Tell me about Elijah."

Then God said "What do you want to know about Elijah? His exploits have been chronicled in My Book. And in some detail too."

I decided just to go for broke on the first question, and I said "Elijah and Elisha. Are they the same person? Seems to me that they are so much alike I can't tell where Elijah leaves off and Elisha begins."

And I couldn't tell whether God was provoked or amused by my question. He said "Where the mantle of Elijah dropped onto the shoulders of Elisha is where the one stops and the other begins. Now you are a father and a grandfather. You ought to understand about things like that."

Then I felt that I had got off on the wrong foot and I said "I just wondered" because I didn't know what else to say.

"Wondering is about your highest virtue," God said. "But indeed both men are credited with a remarkable case of artificial respiration on a widow's son so that might have confused you. Nevertheless, you must remember that there were a lot of widows in Israel in those days and most of them had sons."

"But do all the widows' sons pass out when the prophet comes to dinner?"

"In this case, yes, but I expect that you have a hidden question here somewhere "

Frankly, I had some question in my mind about the prophets spending so much time with the widows who have sickly sons, but I was afraid to ask Him anymore about that. I recalled in my own mind that widows were pointed out in the New Testament as deserving of special attention, and I decided to leave the matter alone because my curiosity might be seen as meddling. Still, I did not feel that God had fully answered my question, but I saw that He had told me as much as He judged that I need to know on the question of prophets and widows and widows' sons, so I went on to the next question that was bothering me. "Drought" I said. "I reckon droughts were fairly common too, and the need for water will drive people to make some big decisions. I was wondering, though, in view of the water shortage, about Elijah digging a ditch and filling it with water there on Mount Carmel when he wanted to show up the priests of Baal for a bunch of frauds."

"Yes. Well, that was definitely the high point in Elijah's life. And high points not only require all the necessary ingredients, but they are usually followed by a depression. But what really interests you right now ..."

He paused and I said "What really happened up there on Mount Carmel when the priests of Baal cut up the way they did and couldn't make a drop of water except for their own sweat, and then Old Elijah got up and called on You and You sent a gully washer."

"That was not just a test for rain makers. It was the dividing line for My People on this business of the Fertility Cult."

"That was mentioned in the theological school when I was studying Old Testament but the professor didn't seem to know any more about it than he needed to know, or else he was not telling all he knew because he was a bit squeamish about the sex part of it."

"More likely he told you more than he did know. Fertility is the key to every thing with people and animals and plants, all of them. I told you that when we talked about the Garden of Eden. And I even alluded to it when I told you about circumcision. But Baalism was a different view of procreation." His voice, or what I took to be His Voice, became intense at this point. "Those priests of Baal were nothing more than religious whoremasters, and they were using their religion just to gratify their sexual desires. I was determined to get rid of it, root and branch, because it was even spilling over into My People's worship of Me, and I didn't rain fire on Sodom and Gomorrah just for a practice run. I meant that to be the end of it, and then it kept cropping up. Even at Shiloh. But there I was able to keep matters under enough control to save the boy Samuel for My use, and he turned out better than anybody else in his time, even though he misunderstood me about wanting to kill everybody. King Saul had his weak points, but Samuel made them worse."

'Well, I still don't understand how the fire fell at the right time to lap up all the water and the sacrificial animal, and then it was followed by a rain that brought the drought to an end. To tell the truth, I wondered where all the water came from to fill up the ditch around the altar. It seemed to me that in a time of water shortage that was an awful waste, certainly if people and animals were thirsty, there must have been a better use for water than filling the moats with it. But I guess that's Your Business, how you wanted to use the water."

"Indeed it is, and if you have read Jesus' reply to the question about the so called waste of the precious ointment on him, you my get the point about the use of the water on Mount Carmel."

After that I kept quiet about the water in the ditch around the altar. I reckoned that if God wanted to use it that way, He knew where there was plenty more if another need arose, and He might just hand me a bucket and tell me to go get it.

I was still curious about how He brought all those events together. It just amazed me, but He said that I could learn a lot from the study of weather and I could save my questions for theological concerns, so I went back to the basic issue of the Fertility Cult, and I said "Well, I have to say that Elijah did certainly lop off root and branch when he slew the four hundred and fifty priests of Baal, but I was disappointed to find that he had cut and run when that witch Queen Jezebel threatened him." I said "She must have had a big stake in that Baal worship. Something more than just a matter of the name of the god."

"You can also say that she had a big stick in her hand when she sent the message to Elijah. She was the High Priestess and although it is not to Elijah's credit that he ran and hid himself, I understand. He was hungry and thirsty and exhausted." There was a hint of humor in His Voice when He said "You might be a bit tired yourself after lopping off four hundred and fifty heads all in one day."

"It just didn't seem consonant with Elijah's fearless character to run and hide "

"You must understand," He said, "that depression follows elation. Besides, if you read the whole story, you will see that after I had put some backbone into Elijah, and he got some food in his stomach, he dealt with Jezebel."

"And I imagine King Ahab was not entirely averse to what happened to his queen. I always had the impression that he was hen pecked and he just did what she told him to do most of the time. I hope he learned his lesson and turned his head around about Baalism."

"Not much hope for King Ahab," the Lord said sadly. "But getting My People straightened out on this matter was very important. It still took Amos and Micah and a few other good prophets to clarify the matter and make people see that I am the One God Who requires ethical and moral behavior of men."

"Well, what really impresses me is that Elijah shows up again in the New Testament. He is on the Mount of Transfiguration with Jesus and Moses, and then the people thought Jesus was calling on him from the cross. I'm surprised that he was not mentioned by the writer to the Hebrews in his roll call of the faithful."

"It was a long list and he just ran out of space, but Elijah's omission from that list takes nothing away from his importance. He struck that decisive blow against the Fertility Cult of Baal, and although My People never get it all out of their system, it is all out of their theology."

"I am glad to get it straight from You, and grateful to Elijah, and glad I don't have to meet him on one of his bad moods. I'll take a lesson from Jezebel."

"You would do better to take a lesson from the story of Elijah's mantle falling on Elisha. It would improve your performance of duties considerably if some of his courage and his loyalty to me would rub off on you. It is good that you want to write these stories about the heroes; it would be better for you to become one."

I was surprised to learn that He even considered me the right material for it and I said "Me a hero?"

Then the Lord's voice became whimsical as he said "You might even take a lesson from that story about Elisha and the boys and the bear, although it is probably apocryphal, you should always show respect for bald heads. There may be more inside them than you realize. You may yet discover that Learning can be heroic."

"Lord, make me a hero, if that's what You want, but I'm not seeking a bullet nor a rope around my neck. Just let it be said that I wrote the best I could."

"I will arrange that," He said. "And if you have written something that you have doubts about ... well, remember the fire. It can lick up an acceptable sacrifice, and it can consume what's not good enough to share with My People."

CHAPTER TWENTY

ABOUT JOB

"What is it now?" God seemed a bit impatient with me, and I did have a sheepish look on my face as I stood there after the interview should have been over. "There seems to be no end to your curiosity about the people who have filled my Book and made it the most read Book in the world. At least, more copies, of it have been bought; whether they have been read is another matter. And even the people who read it do pick and choose. But I can't blame them for that. Some parts are better than others. For instance, the Twenty Third Psalm is worth more than the whole Book of Begats. That's the one where all that genealogy is to be found, and what led to it. Well now, what is it with you this time?"

"Job," I said. "He claimed that you did him in for no good reason. Shafted him is what people today would say. I was wondering why."

God did not reply immediately and I began to feel self conscious about asking when there is already so much said in the Story itself. So of course I had to talk, and I recited the calamaties that had befallen Job. The loss of his sheep and camels and she asses, which I assumed to be of more value than mere he asses. The deaths of his children and all the servants. Seems that with every new misfortune the messenger of bad news was the only one left alive. Then the boils on his own body.

I had a boil on my butt once and it was painful to sit down even on a chair, and I could imagine it was worse on the dung heap."

But then God said that Job had done a creditable job of speaking for himself and that he had summed it all up when he admitted that the Lord only took away from him what He had previously given him. "Good and Evil are the two parts of Life," God told me. "What is there to understand? Where is the mystery?"

"I guess you mean the Forbidden Fruit," I said, as if we had not already talked about the Knowledge of Good and Evil when I asked Him about Adam and Eve.

"I mean there are two forces at work in the world, Good and Evil, and Job encountered both of them in full measure."

"Both of them? Seems to me he must have eaten the bad part and missed out on the good part. He loses it all. His children are killed when the house falls in on them. His wife suggests suicide; that's about as helpful as a swarm of locusts. And those friends of his. I am speaking of Eliphas the Temanite and Bildad the Shuhite and Zophan the Naamanite, not to mention that young smart ass who showed up late in the show. With friends like that Job didn't need any enemies. But it seems he had One. The Arch Enemy. Satan. I reckon he is the old Serpent done sprouted legs."

"Hold it." God had put His Hand up in front of my face. "This World which you are about to bad mouth. It's the only one capable of sustaining human life, as far as you know. But maybe you would like to go along. on the next flight to Mars."

"I was only saying that Job seems to have had all the bad luck," I said weakly.

"Yes, so it seems to you. But just remember. He could not have lost all those camels if he didn't have them. Same for the sheep and the she asses. And his seven sons and three daughters. Think of the people in this world who don't have one camel. One sheep. One she ass. One son or one daughter. And as for his wife, I left her there for a purpose. A man is never. entirely a lone if he has a wife, even if she does Make unacceptable suggestions about solving his problems."

"I can see what You mean about that, but Job's friends. Now I have some dillies, and I admit it, but mostly they refrain from pointing out all my faults unless they have had too many beers. Job's friends even make up faults for him that he never heard of. I don't reckon they expected ever to be invited back to Job's house. And so persistent in their efforts. Long winded. How they could talk so much without even mentioning the good things Job had done is a mystery to me. I'll bet he never even got a chance to get a whiff of the aroma of the dung heap while his friends were consoling him."

"It is clear that Job knew he was on the manure pile, and he had time to scratch his boils while his friends talked. But that is not the issue in this drama."

"Well, just for the record, I would like to know what the issue is."

"The issue is that a Good Man just naturally attracts the attention of a Bad Man who just has to hit on him because he is a Good Man and it makes the Bad Man feel good to see the Good Man suffer."

"Thanks a lot for that. It makes me feel better to know that I won't be a magnet for the Bad Guys to hit on me because they won't even notice me."

"So much the worse for you; I will notice you."

Now that was about as comforting as the hugs and kisses of Job's friends, so I said "Where does the Devil, the fellow called Satan, come in here anyway? According to the Book, he has been wandering around the country looking for trouble and when he comes to the monthly staff meeting to give his report to You, he sounds about like the radio announcer for the local funeral home who sadly announced to his listeners that he had no obituaries to report this morning but he hoped to have some tomorrow."

"Your sense of humor is commendable if not saving. Now, the Devil, or Satan as you know, is the Evil part of your own nature."

"Maybe I did know that, but I believe that I would have felt better about myself if I had not known it."

"It's people like you," God said, "who invent the Devil to escape their own personal responsibility for the bad things they do. By saying The Devil made me do it, you can shift the blame onto some Evil Force that is too great for you to resist. Hence you can't be held responsible, and you hope you can escape the obligation to pay up. Don't kid yourself. Every man has eaten the fruit of the Knowledge of Good and Evil. And trying to deny it by conjuring up a super human instigator only worsens your case."

"Well, it does seem to me that what started out to be an inquiry into the sufferings of Job has now become a very personal indictment. But I guess I asked for it. Anyway, I still have the question about a Good Man suffering unjustly, so to speak, which is to say that far from his punishment fitting. the crime, the crime is being inflicted on him by others who either claim to be blameless, or at least have been appointed as prosecutor and executioner to carry out the work of affliction on the poor sufferer who is baffled by it all and is made to feel resentful, and rightly so, by the injustice of it."

"And this is true. But you refuse to see that Evil simply flourishes in the face of Good and then becomes a challenge to the Good Man to confront and overthrow the Evil. Think of the effect on My Son Jesus when He walked into the Temple, My Temple, and saw it being desecrated by the greed of the merchants of sacrifice there. He was so incensed by what He saw that He kicked over the money changers' tables and drove the offenders out with a whip. But they came back and hanged Him on a cross because of what He had done. He had exacerbated the Evil in them, and they vented it on HIM."

"I reckon then that You are going to tell me that Job was Your Old Testament Christ."

"You guessed it. And Prometheus was my Greek mythical Christ."

"But at the end You evened up the score for Job. He wound up with a new wife and ten more children, which I might question as a bonus in his old age, and more camels than a man would need unless he was doing a desert transport business. And enough sheep to clothe in wool half the people in his part of the country."

"Right. And My Son Jesus sits at My Right Hand on the Throne of Heaven, so to speak. And even Prometheus was eventually released from the rock. So you must try to realize that I am still in control. And that is what Job learned. I know it is not a satisfactory answer, but there is no promise of satisfaction with the results of eating the fruit of the Tree of the Knowledge of Good and Evil. Unless you find your satisfaction in a good fight in which you are bound to get bloodied. But I will be waiting there in your corner with a towel to wipe away the blood from your face, and to say to you Good Boy. You fought a good fight and ..."

"I know. I read what Paul said, but I still think Job deserved better than just a replacement of the wife he had got used to, and children he would have to train up all over again, and camels with mean tempers and sheep and she asses which I don't claim to know about."

"I am the most patient of Gods," He said "because I am the only God, and I bear the complaints of my children with grace and patience, but don't push Me too far."

"Well, I still think You ought to afflict those three friends of Job, Bildad and Company with boils, and let their camels bite them on their way home, and have their wives to meet them with bad news like Where have you been out gallivanting about over the country while I am stuck here with squalling younguns and everything."

Well, God always has the last word, of course, and this time He really surprised me by quoting a quatrain that some poet with the wisdom of Job had written:

Truth is ever on the scaffold, evil ever on the throne

But that scaffold rules the future, for beyond the dim unknown

God is standing in the shadows

Ever watching over His own.

Then I realized He had answered my question and I hoped it even helped old Job.

CHAPTER TWENTY ONE

ABOUT JONAH AND THE FISH

After God had cleared up the mystery of the flood for me I was still in one of my curious moods that sent the message to Him that I wanted to know more He said "Now what is it you want to know?" And I said "About Jonah and the whale I've ..."

"Fish," He said. "I never said it was a whale. Try to get this right at the outset. A whale is an air breathing mammal that gives birth to babies and then suckles them the way other mammals do. Closer kin to you than the fishes are. No account of a whale ever swallowing a man, although Moby Dick would have been justified in swallowing Captain Ahab."

"All right then, Jonah and the Big Fish. I still want to know what happened. I have swallowed a lot of big fish tales but this one about the fish Swallowing Jonah takes the prize and I've never heard the inside story."

"Whales prefer plankton to people in their diet," He said. "That is just to get the matter of it being a fish and not a whale squared away ... Now, what is it you want to know about Jonah?"

"Well, three days inside the fish. That's a long time, and a lot can happen in three days. Not to speak of digestive juices. I'll just assume that You had arranged comfortable living quarters for Jonah. I don't reckon he would expect air conditioning and television since those little conveniences had not been invented yet. But my question is "Just what did Jonah do in there? How did he spend his time during those three days?"

"With Me, mostly. And in conversation. For you must understand that Jonah was a lot like you. He had a lot to learn, and it took three days for him to learn enough to set up shop and do a fair job of preaching."

"And You had a special job of preaching for him to do?"

"I had given him a commission to Nineveh. It turned out that I had picked him green, and he was not ready for Nineveh."

'Not ready. Now there is something I had not considered.. But now that You mention it, I spent six years in theological school, getting ready to preach, and when I got out, thinking I knew it all, I still put my foot in my mouth on the racial issue in Georgia, and a lot of people there thought I didn't know my ..."

"Never mind about that. We will just say you were a slow learner. Or, to be kind to you we will say Georgia was not ready for you. But I gave Jonah a Three Day Crash Course, and if you have read the end of the story you will see that he still didn't get it right. Which leads me to believe that Man's name of Homo Sapiens could just drop the Sapiens part because he is not as wise as he ought to be."

"Right. I get the point. But about the Three Days. I believe You implied that there was a lot of close communing going on there in the fish's belly."

"It's not necessary to say Right when you acknowledge something I have said. We will just talk about the Three Days which I will call Day One, Day Two, and Day Three."

"Ri ... Well, Day One must have been a shocker for Jonah. He's been hiding out in the hold of the ship, and a big storm comes up and the ship is about to sink, and he gets blamed for it all and the sailors pitch him overboard and he's swallowed up by this ... Big Fish."

"Now you are right. And the first thing I had to do was calm Jonah down and let him know that I was right there with him, and that I understood how he felt."

"How did he feel?"

"Scared. There is no other word for it. Jonah was scared witless, and that's where I started in with his instruction. Fear. Fear was at the root of his trouble. I had given him a big job to do over there at Nineveh and he just plain was not up to it because he was afraid. He lacked confidence. Didn't believe that he could pull it off. Scared. That's where he was."

"Well then, how did You deal with that? You find this fellow in the belly of a fish. He's water soaked from a recent dip in the ocean, he's sniveling over his bad fortune. It's dark in there and I assume that makes matters worse because he's probably scared of the dark. Then You come and that probably made him tremble. How DID you deal with his fear?"

"You are wrong about one part of the cause of his fear. I let him know that I was right there with him, for surely you must know that the real basis of fear is the feeling that you are all alone and there's nobody to talk to, nobody to listen or to say a word of comfort, and nobody to hold your hand. And you are the person credited with saying that what you did when you were a chaplain was hold people's hands. But Jonah. There wasn't even a Ninevite nor a heathen sailor there with him. He was all alone. Except for Me. And at first he was so scared he didn't even realize that I was there. I had to pull his ear to get his attention. That's just a figure of speech, pulling his ear, but not a bad figure of speech, I made it; everything I made is good. For something. Even crocodiles."

I started to say that I had not actually bad mouthed crocodiles to the extent of ruling out their place in the ecosystem, just that I ... but He said "I heard what you said about the crocodiles. Now you will do well to just stay out of the water where the crocodiles are. Now, back to Jonah. That First Day."

"Right," I said, forgetting. "Day One. Tell me about that First Day."

"We spent Day One dealing with Jonah's fear, and when he dozed off that first night he had it about whipped. He had survived the storm and the pitching into the sea and the being swallowed up, and now he had got his bearings even in the dark because I was a Light to him. Oh, it was still dark in there, but it was different because he could feel Me near him. He would say things like Stay close, and Hold my hand. And by the time Day One ended and we had the Fear Factor under control we were ready for Day Two which was going to be rough because this Jonah was one angry man.

"Yes, he had dried out and warmed up, but that was just it. He was too warm. Hot. Seething with anger. Out of control when I brought up the subject of his mission to the Ninevites. Oh, he hated them with a passion. I do believe that if he had discovered that a Ninevite had been slipped into that fish's belly in the darkness, he would have attacked him and tried to choke him. He had forgotten what it was to be lonely, and one Ninevite in there with him would have been one person too many.

"He hated the people of Nineveh that much, and he just could not understand why I would send him on a preaching mission to Nineveh, of all places."

"It's a mystery to me too, "I said. "And it's one of the things I was going to ask You about. Not that I feel that You have to explain Your actions to me, but just that I don't understand. Seems to me that he could find plenty of sinners to preach to right there in Israel where he was without having to go to the ends of the earth to find someone. Amos did."

"Never you mind about Amos. He had his job and he did it well. At least he got about half way through his sermon before they sent him back to the hills. But yes, I had a special reason for sending Jonah to Nineveh. And that is what made him so angry."

"And why was he so angry at the people of Nineveh? What had they done to him?"

"This may be too complicated for you, but I will try to make it clear and simple. Nineveh was a great power. Military might. Wealth. Prestige. Nineveh was like, well, like Britain was when my man Ghandi was preaching. Nineveh was like the United States is now. Big. Powerful. And Proud. I know you have seen those bumper stickers. I'm proud to be an American. And Jonah was a little nobody from nowhere. He was a Jew over there in that little powerless state of Israel, and he didn't even hold an office there. Not even a bureau chief for the newspaper.

"I'm telling you. Being a nobody makes a man hate the guts of the Big Boys. That little nobody is willing to strap a bomb to his body and blow himself up in order to take a few of the Big Boys with him into oblivion. Well, that was Jonah. Full of hatred for the Ninevites. And that was Day Two."

"What did You say to him?"

"Say to him? What can even God say to a man who is full of hatred? It was what I DID to him, what I had to DO to him, as you will note from what has already been written in the Big Fish Story. But what I had to SAY to him is that even Ninevites are my people too. Sinners? Yes. Big Sinners. But I want to save them too. And if I can just bring them to repentance..."

Believe me, Patient Reader, It's a real experience to hear God get emotional about people He wants to save. Maybe you've heard Billy Graham make his appeal for sinners to fill the aisles. Maybe you've heard the candidates for President talk about their concern for hard working middle class people being taxed to death. Maybe you've even heard a good woman make her case for a good for nothing husband, or a mother make her plea for a wayward son or daughter. But if you have not heard God make His case for saving the whole human race and especially the little people who become terrorists, you haven't lived. God can pour it on. He can do it for Caesar; he can do it for the lowliest slave.

Maybe you think God is not concerned about what this war we are in now in Iraq and Afghanistan and all over the world, what it is doing to the boys over there kicking in doors and dragging people out into the street and pushing over houses where they think a terrorist maybe hiding. But here I am stealing God's line because He and I have been talking so much lately I forget where He leaves off and I begin, so maybe I'll just let Him speak to Jonah because it is now Day Two in the fish's belly.

"I tried to make Jonah see that the people of Nineveh were just like the people back home, only more of them, and better equipped with heavy armor but poor lost devils all the same."

Day Three: I said "Tell me about Day Three. That must have been the Big Day. I know how You are about doing things in three days."

God said "Day Three was both the Day of Hope and the Day of Disappointment."

"How could that be? It seems contradictory."

"Contradictions. Paradoxes. Call them what you will. Nothing in this world is one sided. And certainly not inside a fish's belly. I thought I had Jonah ready for the job. He was going out there and preach repentance to Nineveh, and he did, for you must see that the Third Day was when he was belched up onto the shore and it seemed he was really going to get it right this time. He was a hell fire and damnation preacher too. He just scared hell out of the Ninevites. Especially when he gave his own personal testimony. Told them about the storm at sea and being swallowed by the fish. Anyway, they repented in sackcloth and ashes - that is just a figure of speech to you - and it was a revival to make old Billy Sunday blush for shame.

"But then Jonah himself fouled it all up. He was displeased with his own success The results of his own preaching. He sat down and sulked because I didn't rain fire and brimstone on the Ninevites the way he had threatened that I would do. Why, this numbskull couldn't recognize success when it reared up and looked him in the face. And I had to teach him another lesson. What you might call a post graduate course, but it was really all part of the Third Day, the way I see Days because I used a gourd vine and a worm to teach him a lesson that anybody with a grain of sense should have been able to see without an object lesson But then, I have to admit that I pick some real dillies to do my work for me.

"Old Paul was right about that and one of the best examples of what he said Peter was a match for him too. And just look at John Calvin and Martin Luther. And Savonarola. Now there's one for the book You could pick some of your own contemporaries. Or, if you have the courage, you can even look in the mirror.

"Hey, I may even have a little job for Pat Robertson yet. Nothing is impossible for Me."

"I believe, Lord, help Thou mine unbelief."

CHAPTER TWENTY TWO

About John the Baptist

I was pondering over some of those characters I had discussed with God, and I thought: We have talked about all those mythic and legendary figures from the Old Testament. Even some historical ones, allowing for the theological bias of the historian. And I have been afraid to tackle the ones in the New Testament. Is it because I am seeing the New Testament the way those old Jews saw the Ark of the Covenant? Something too holy for me to touch? Is that it?

And before I could answer my own question about myself, God spoke and said to me "That is it. You are afraid. But fear not. I am with you. And I am the same God who called Abraham out into a strange land, and stopped him from sacrificing Isaac. I am the same God who wrestled with Jacob, and made a man, even a Prince of him. I am the same God who spoke to Noah when he was building that big ship to save a little bit of My Creation. I am even the same God who spoke to Adam and Eve in the Garden, and created a Man there."

I was startled by His Coming to me this way, and all I could say was "But Lord, those Old Testament characters were different, and I didn't have to admit fully they even existed, factually, historically, I mean. But now we are getting too close to home when we start talking about Jesus."

And God said "Absolutely " He surprised me there too because I had been heard to say that when people say "Absolutely" they haven't really looked at what they are talking about. But when God said "absolutely" I knew He knew what He was talking about. And He was sure God Absolute about Jesus.

But then He surprised me again by saying "But we have to talk about John first. Remember John? That strange character out there in the wild places, preaching Repentance and baptizing people in the Jordan River?

"You Baptists even took your name from the practice of baptizing. Yes, you took the name Baptist and then you forgot about John. But now you have to remember: John the Baptist, the Baptizer, the Forerunner of My Son, preparing a road for Him in the wilderness, letting the people, even the religious leaders, know what to expect when My Son would appear on the scene."

God seemed to be enjoying my discomfort, and He showed no sign of letting up on me. "Telling it like it was. Laying it on the line. Calling names. Sparing nobody. Preaching his way right into prison, and laying his head on the platter. All for the sake of presenting My Son to the world."

I finally found my tongue, and I stammered. "Yes, Lord, and when I see him, hear him, feel his hot breath on my neck, I think old Amos has come down out of the hills again. I think Elijah is calling down fire on the altar. I think even old Samuel ..."

"Yes," the Lord said. "And I want you to feel it. But I want you to know too that even John did not know the full story on My Son. I could tell you that even My Son did not know it all until that final gasp. It is finished. That's why I gave them that story about the forty days in the wilderness, and the temptation by the devil, so that they, and you, would know what He went through, from the Baptism at John's hands to the Crucifixion at Pontius Pilate's.

"By the way," the Lord said, as if to lighten my load for just a moment: "It was right clever of you to come up with those letters, the correspondence with Rome. But don't let it go to your head. That's just the way inspiration works. You just remember where it all comes from; that's why, I want to talk with you about John now."

"I don't know where we are going here Lord," I said. "I know John got into trouble with the same crowd that did Jesus in. But I am not sure I am connecting the dots."

"All right, when Jesus was challenged by that crowd, as you call them, he answered by putting the question to them: "John, was he from God or from men? Did he speak for God or for men? Was his baptism - and remember that it was his baptism that launched My Son on his mission - was his baptism of God or Men?"

I said "I am beginning to get Your Drift. But maybe You had better lay the Holy Ghost on me if You want me to understand You completely. Yes, Maybe I need that baptism with the Holy Ghost ... and with fire, because I seem to be in over my head in these waters. I just can't see where we are coming from nor where we are heading."

"All right." God became more patient with me now. He seemed to realize that it was more than I could take in, and He was going to spoon feed me. "Remember what John said when the Big Boys from Jerusalem tried to pen him down about what they should do? He said You have two shirts and you see your brother naked. You give one of your shirts to him. Luckily, they did not ask about two naked men, for John would have told them to give both shirts. Now here was a man who was clothed in animal skins and his loins tied up with a leather thong and not even a brass buckle. And he is not asking for a shirt for himself. He is telling them to give their shirt to the poor, the naked, the destitute, the dispossessed of the land. And don't you forget for one moment that the goods of this world are still disproportionately divided between the haves and the have nots and your people, your country, your nation, which claims Me for their God, are concerned because some of the wealth of America is going now to the poor people of other nations, and they can't keep it all for themselves forever. But they have got to have it all. And keep it all. And to hell with the naked people of the earth!"

"So that's how he lost his head?"

"That. And the woman who tricked King Herod."

"Yes, now tell me about that. Had John laid such a guilt trip on her that she just had to have his head. Or was she just that mean and power hungry?"

"There's not much difference in your two questions. It was her hunger for power, the need to be close to power, and then to manipulate that power, to wrap her body in that power, that drove her to do the things that made her guilty. And she could not bear the guilt; she had to strike at the man who called her guilt to her mind and the attention of the nation."

"So what about John's own loneliness and despair when he lay in prison waiting to have his head chopped off, and he wondered if he had been wrong about the whole thing? And he sent messengers to Jesus to ask, to, verify, to get the stamp of approval, to know if what he had said really had come from You? To know if the One he had baptized really was the Messiah come to deliver his people. To know the message of Repentance had not been wasted because the One for Whom he had prepared the way was the Real Prince Who was to walk on that road and to declare the Coming of the Kingdom of Heaven on Earth?"

"Yes, and do you remember what My Son answered to John's question?"

"Go tell John what you have seen. The people being healed and restored to hope?"

"That's it, essentially."

"But did that satisfy John?"

"Probably not. But he himself had declared Jesus' superiority to him in every way. He could not complain if Jesus had gone beyond him, or in a different direction."

"Then Jesus got into trouble with the very same people who had rejected John's message."

"He did indeed. As both He and John might well have expected."

"And what if the religious leaders of Israel had answered Jesus' question and said "John was from God?"

"Then they would have had to say that Jesus was from God."

"And then what?"

"Then Israel would have been saved."

"But they didn't."

"And so I had to start over with the Remnant, the Brand plucked from the fire. The Church. But that was nothing new for Me. I had done it before. Remember Noah. Abraham. All the rest. Now do I have to start all over again now and here?"

"You are asking me, Lord?"

"Yes, I am asking you, because I am putting this question to you: Are you willing to lay it - your head if necessary - on the line to turn My People around and get them back on the right path?

"Or do I have to come with Fire and thoroughly cleanse the threshing floor and start all over again?"

"Oh Lord," I cried. "Surely You don't expect me to ..."

"Am I not talking to you? What was it your favorite author Hemingway said? If you hear the tolling of the bell, ask not for whom the bell tolls. The bell tolls for you."

CHAPTER TWENTY THREE

ABOUT JESUS THE CHRIST

I guess I thought I was just working up to the real question when I was talking with God about Peter and Paul. Especially after all those Old Testament characters. Because the question I really wanted to ask Him was about Jesus. He was the One Who holds me in wonder and surprise and mystery and any other condition than just the ordinary. So after much hesitation, I worked myself up to it. And I said "God, will You tell me about Jesus?"

His answer was not a simple Yes or No. He said "You are asking Me to tell you about Jesus? I sent Him to you to tell you about Me."

That set me back on my heels, so to speak, thinking about God and Jesus and me, and I said "But God, there is still so much about Him that I don't understand. And the more I read of what has been written about Him, and the more I listen to what people say about Him, the more the picture is confused, and how am I ever going to get to first base in this game if I am dependent on Him now to tell me about You? Can't You just tell me who He is?"

I guess God was disappointed in me. He had expected something better of me after all the conversations we had carried on about the characters in His Book. So He jerked me up onto my feet with His own question. "All right then," God said. "You are going to make it a game of chasing mystery round and round. What is it about Jesus that you don't understand?"

I said "Well, to start with, what is this story about the Virgin Birth? I've read all the old Greek myths and the myths of just about all the people who have ever lived on Earth, and they all have stories about gods and women and goddesses and men, and the Church teaches that Jesus was born of a virgin by the Holy Ghost which seems to be a stand in for You just to remove the need for a human father. And they have brought the Holy Ghost into it to make it appear that Mary became pregnant because the Wind blew on her." I was about out of breath myself, but I drew a lung full again and went on. "And it even looks like, if You will excuse the implication here, that Joseph got cuckolded, and then the whole world, or at least the most of the people in the Church, must brag about it, and I've even had people tell me that unless I believe that Jesus was conceived in some mysterious manner that obviates the need for a human father, He couldn't be the Son of God, and if I don't believe that He was born that way, I could go to hell. Now what do You think of that?"

I got all of that out in one big breath because I was afraid that if I paused for one moment I might lose my courage and back away from the question. And then when I did get another breath, I said "And I did so much want to believe that I am a son of God, or at least stand a chance of becoming a son of God, Your son, and there was my old man, my very human father, Papa, no less, horny and proud as I know he was, standing in my way. Now what am I to make of that?"

I could swear that while I was getting all of this out, God had a smug sort of smile on His Face, although of course I couldn't see His Face, but in my mind's eye I could see the artist's impression of the Face of Jesus. He had long dark hair and a beard and piercing eyes, sometimes blue and sometimes dark. And He was not smiling, but He looked as if He might be friendly and compassionate. Very manly looking in a handsome way but nothing pretty like the movie stars. And then God said "You have become so imbued with those old myths that you are in danger of confusing Me with Zeus or some other unsavory character out of the Orient or Africa.

"Where were you standing when John baptized Jesus, and I spoke to Him so loud that people thought it was thunder? Where have you been all the time I have tried to tell you the mystery of creation and procreation and the holy union of Man and Woman?"

I said "I'm trying Lord. You might even say I'm hoping. But it all seems too big for me, and too good to be true. Is Jesus really Your Son?"

Then God said "of course, Jesus of Nazareth, the child of Joseph and Mary, is My Son, and you are My Son, without impugning the sanctity of your parents' marriage. Jesus is called the First Born, and Unique Son because He is the First to really get the message from Me and the one who perfectly reflects My true Character in contradiction if this will help you with my Old Testament characters to Samuel, and you can be, indeed you are My son, a younger Brother to Jesus. And certainly you are flawed a bit as I have tried to point out to you without discouraging your efforts at sonship. But you are no less My Son, and all the others who seek My Face as Jesus did, and then in turn reflect My Face to the world of men and women struggling and striving for a place in the sun; all these are My children, My sons and daughters, and don't you be put off by the people who want to evade the responsibilities of sonship by relegating it to some area of magic and mystery beyond the knowledge and experience of man."

God paused for just a moment, and then he said "People do that in order to make it seem impossible to do what they are not willing to do."

I said "What is that, Lord?" And He said "Be like Jesus. They excuse themselves by making Him different in nature, hence incapable of being the example of character and behavior that I am requiring them to follow."

I was standing agape with wonder when God said "Virgin Birth. All it takes for a Virgin Birth is a Love Pure and without doubt or question. Add to that a Third Person, Me, and you have a son of God born of a loving union of trust between Man and Woman. Those old Greeks who stood around the walls of Troy, bragging about their ancestry and claiming that Zeus had slipped off from Hera to chase down some mortal girl were just trying to cover up something that can't be covered because nothing is more obvious than a pregnancy unless it's what caused the pregnancy."

I started to stammer out something about Southern Baptists even refusing to send men and women to the mission field unless they signed an oath that they believe in the Virgin Birth and God just laughed and said, "You Southern Baptists have tried My Patience since the days of slavery. One of these days I am going to …" But He stopped there, leaving me wondering what He is going to do to us Baptists.

It was just as well for me that he did stop there because I wanted to get on to the next question. It was one that just naturally followed after God had declared that Jesus was His Son at His Baptism. So I said "Well, now, about the Forty Days of Temptation in the Wilderness, when Satan came and offered Jesus all those good things that must have looked so good to Him. I am pleased to note that he didn't try to bribe Him with Wine and Women the way the sports scouts do the young athletes. But just what did happen there? I would certainly like to have it straight from You because I suspect that I've been given a snow job on that one too."

"Be more specific," God advised me. "Just what is it that you want to know?"

"Well, I would just like to know if this was real, or if it is a sort of parable like the ones Jesus Himself was known to tell when He was speaking of things difficult for people to understand. Were these temptations presented Him in just this way? Or do I have to look for hidden meaning presented in obscure ways."

"Now you are becoming more and more indefinite about it," God said. "So I will just come out of the mists of your obscurity and tell you that the temptation is a telescoping of His whole ministry. Yes, He was tempted to get where He was going by being a miracle worker. What could be more spectacular than walking on water? As He discovered His own healing powers, He was tempted to meet head on the sufferings and the pains and the sickness of mankind, and win over a grateful and adoring following that would be as devoted to him as the ones who saw His miracles were admiring. And yes, when He felt the surge of the people on the Road to Jerusalem all crying out for a Messiah who would bring again the Kingdom of David, He felt what your Presidential hopefuls feel here in America. But in the end, He saw it wouldn't work. It was all a road to nowhere but disappointment and failure and bitterness. It had been tried and had failed."

"Then the temptation was not real like it says there?"

"Of course it was real. More real than it is presented in the story. Real in the sense that He was finding that He could really do those things. They became real possibilities in the actual experience with men. How much more real do you think it can get? I want you to get REAL about My Son and His ministry and stop the child's play."

God paused for a moment, and then I realized that what I had said about it not being real had displeased Him. He said "It's the people who put it all in an idealistic setting of a hungry man in the desert facing the devil, yes, it's these people who make it unreal. If you want Reality, it has to take place in the context of possibility, and all of that took place in His ministry, right down to the cleansing of the Temple in Jerusalem."

"So what about those miracles? Was He really a Wonder Worker? We saw magicians in Egypt. Elijah had to deal with them on the mountain. Was Jesus just another magician? Smoke and mirrors?"

"His was a magnetic and powerful personality. He was indeed the Master of the World, pushing the bounds of possibility. But it is possible to feed the hungry. If those who have more than they need to eat will share with the ones who hunger. It is possible to heal the sick and the wounded ... if you care enough about them. Possible to walk on water. Calm the raging sea. Haul in a great catch of fish. If man's potential for harnessing the forces of nature to serve the needs of others is fully realized with practical programs of help."

"I fear that I am becoming more confused than ever. Is this all just a form of rationalization?"

"Very well. The world, as one of your philosophers has said, is what you see, And what Jesus did in many of his acts was what the people saw Him do. Even what He saw Himself doing. You just need to get your eyes opened so that you can see what He is doing in the world today "

"Yes Lord, but raising the dead? Lazarus?"

"Now you are getting into the area of spiritual reality. I thought you would never get there. Congratulations." He seemed to be toying with me, but I kept quiet, waiting to know what He would say to the question of raising Lazarus. "Yes, Jesus brought people who were essentially dead to Life again. So powerful was His influence on people that they came to a new experience of Life that can only be expressed in terms of a resurrection. Well, John did it very well when he wrote about being born again." He paused for this to soak in. Then. "Do you think the world would have heard of the humble home of Mary, Martha and Lazarus if Jesus had not entered it and changed Death into Life?"

I was staring off into space again. Trying to recall my vision of God's Face when He said "Can you come up with a better term for the difference Jesus made in that little family of Mary, Martha and Lazarus? Can you now? If you can, you will be recognized as a gifted theologian. But of course you will be controversial."

I couldn't think of a better term, so that relegated me to a place of mediocrity among theologians, but it gave me a certain immunity to criticism. But I was afraid we were going to get into the matter of Jesus' own resurrection and I was not ready for this yet. Nevertheless, I was about to ask out of sheer wonder if this was what was meant by Jesus' Resurrection, but God said "You have seen Mel Gibson's picture of the Crucifixion. It's called the Passion of the Christ."

I had seen it but I didn't think Mel Gibson's Passion of the Christ had added anything substantial to the Biblical Story. What was bothering me was the Church's interpretation of the Crucifixion. I said "What did Jesus do on the cross?"

"You don't want to hear from Me what the Church Fathers have been telling you for two millennia, I hope."

"No Lord. Spare me that. I have been told that He was suffering under Your Hand to reconcile the world to You by assuaging Your Anger at all of us sinners who would ever live and sin and all be forgiven and go to heaven because He bore our sins on the cross. No Lord, I don't believe that and I am hoping for something better from You."

"Then what do you want to hear from me? Something unheard of?"

"Is that too much to hope for? I want to know what was really happening there."

"He was engaging the forces of Evil in mortal combat, and it actually seemed that the Evil forces had won out over Him because they had nailed Him to the Cross. But that was only seeming; it was not the reality. No. The reality was that He had triumphed over the Evil Forces because He had endured all they could pour onto Him. Even Death. And He proved faithful to the very End, exerting the force of Good over Evil, of Forgiveness over Hatred, Fear and Cruelty. That was the Finish that He declared from the Cross."

"And the Resurrection? Was that His final triumph over the Forces of Evil?"

"I have just now told you that the triumph took place on the Cross. So if you can understand Me, the Resurrection, for Him, was already there. It did not have to wait three days as you count time."

"So what was the Resurrection? In terms I can understand where I stand in time?"

"For you, the Resurrection was the coming to life again of His Little Body of Believers. His Church. Peter, James and John, and the other disciples. Mary and the other women. The Church Triumphant is the Risen body of Jesus My Son and Messiah."

"Then this is why they were able to see Him, recognize Him, walk and talk with Him, Even break bread with Him?"

"Yes. Because They were His Risen Body. His Presence alive in the world. They were seeing themselves for the first time in Him. Their new, Risen Selves "

"Oh God! This is different from what people here believe. If I go out and say this to them?"

"They won't believe you. They may give you the smile of tolerance and the frown of disapproval. Does this matter to you more than knowing the Truth?"

"No, Lord. I guess not. But what is this about a Return? Did He really promise to come back?"

"He did, and He did."

"What does that mean?"

"It means He promised and He kept His promise. He is here. All around you. Wherever a child is loved and listened to. Wherever the hungry excite your concern and are fed. Wherever the naked make you feel their nakedness and you clothe them. And the sick are healed and the prisoners set free. Wherever Good engages Evil and overcomes it. Wherever, whenever, however the Spirit of My Son finds a lodging place in men who seek the Truth that sets them free, He has come back in triumph to rule in the world of men."

"Then the Kingdom of Heaven has come on Earth?"

"If you have eyes to see it. Ears to hear it. Hands to touch it. Then the King is here, and where the King is, there is His Kingdom."

"Great God. I'll bet my friends will be surprised when I tell them this."

"Let Us hope you still have a few friends after you tell them what I have shown you."

I came back and said "That's all? That's it? No washing away of my sins on the cross? No gathering up of my bones on Judgment Day? No Return on clouds with armies of angels?"

"I have spoken. You write it."

I said "But Lord..."

He said "Write."

A Post Script

The Romans viewed Jesus as religious fanatic, probably harmless but possibly capable of causing a great deal of trouble because of the Jews who saw Him as a real threat to their way of life, one capable of upsetting the balance of power they had achieved with Rome. So together, Rome acquiescing to the Jews insistent demand, they killed him, both of them thinking that would put an end to the matter.

Within a hundred years Christianity had supplanted Judaism, and within three hundred years, had conquered Rome.

CHAPTER TWENTY FOUR

About the Third Day

"The Third Day. The Third Day," I said, addressing myself to God Who had not asked for my opinion about one day or another. But I was insistent in my query.

"I notice that it was on the third day of Creation that You pulled off the Biggie about all those good things that appeared on the Earth to make it a place fit for a man to live in. Some people think the sixth day was it because you made Man then. And still others put a lot of store by the seventh day when you sat down and just rested, looking at what You had done. But the way I see it, if You hadn't done what You did on the third day, the sixth and seventh days would have been useless."

"I am glad to see that you are that perceptive. It should make you more active in preserving the environment of this Earth."

That made me self conscious about my neglect of the world about me, but I was on an other tangent. So I said "And now We have Jesus rising from the dead on the Third Day. I would just like to know what that means because I have heard a lot of preaching on the subject that just didn't seem to make any sense to me. So I am, coming to You, and asking just what is the meaning of it all. How come Jesus was in the tomb three days instead of Seven, which is another one of Your favorites, or Forty, which seems to get a lot of preference on your calendar."

"And just what was happening during those Three Days? And in particular, what makes the Third Day so special that all Christendom is built on that Third Day. And You certainly can't hear an Easter sermon that does not make a big issue of Jesus coming forth from the tomb on the Third Day. So it must have some special meaning for You."

"Then just what is it that you want to know about the Third Day. I get bored with the prayers of people who can't be definite about what they want, and will not be specific about confessing their sins. One of the most tiresome is the phrase Forgive us our many, many sins. So let's hear it from you now. What?"

"All right. Just what was happening in those Three Days when Jesus was dead? I've read this story about him going to hell to convert the lost souls there. But frankly, that sounds like ... well, like something made up to fit a pattern of some sort. Like writing history to fit one's theology."

"Good Man. No, we can get down to the nitty gritty, as people like to call the reality of a tough situation. It was what I was doing in those Three Days that was so important. The body of Jesus of Nazareth is not really at issue here. But I was doing something creative with His friends and His followers, the men and women who had built their hopes on Him and then had those hopes dashed to the ground when they saw Him hanging dead on the cross."

"And what WERE You doing? That's what I really want to know."

"Well, it was like the First Day of Creation, to use a term that may have some meaning for you. When I was creating Day and Night. Sun, Moon, and Stars. Light. In other words. And world of living things unlike anything else that you may know about in the whole universe "

"I guess I am getting a little glimmer of the Light myself. But I don't see the whole picture clear and in depth."

"No. You don't. But listen here. I was giving eyes and ears and voice to those poor men and women struck blind and deaf and dumb by what had happened to them when Jesus died. I was creating in them the ability to see wonders they had not known existed. To hear sounds they did not know about. And to stand up and speak things that would astound the people in their world."

"I'm trying to follow You, but ..."

"All right. I was giving to those women who came to the tomb the ability to see Jesus as they had never seen Him before. To hear Him as they had never heard Him before. And the men too, the disciples who came running at the news. It was a struggle for them; it was struggling to be born again. But I made new men of them on that third morning after His death. Oh, you could say Third Day, but I had started in on them as soon as they saw Him on the cross. Time. Well, it took a little more time with some of them. You take those two on the road to Emmaus.

"Well, if you want to take a real hard nut to crack, take Saul of Tarsus. Now there was one that took some creative doing on My part. Had to knock him down with a thunderbolt, just to get his attention. Had to blind him with Light to enable him to see. Had to let the thunder roll to get his ears in condition to hear what I wanted to say to him. But once I had him, the New Man, the New Creation, Paul, then I had an instrument in My Hands for overpowering the Roman Empire. Now you listen here to Me. It was the Church that was born, that came to Life, experienced the Resurrection on that Third Day. The Church is His Body, and when that Body arose from the death bed of fear and doubt and despair, I had set a whole new Force loose upon the world. And that world would never be the same again."

There was a tremor in God's voice now as He spoke. Or it seemed to me that I was hearing Him as I had not heard Him before when He was speaking to me about Noah and some of those Old Testament characters. There was the element of pride when He continued. "Did it in Three Days too. Rebuilt that Temple of the Holy Spirit, and created a World in which nothing is impossible for Man. And every thing is Holy for the New Man because My Hand has touched Man's World and made it New and Holy."

"But these men, they were scared and hiding and denying that they even knew Him."

"Ha. I put backbone in them. Let's say I created a new backbone for them. Just look at old Simon Peter. Before and After. Now surely you didn't entirely waste those years in theological school. So that you can't see what I did there in Three Days. But maybe you did. I've been looking at what they are teaching in the theological schools now, and it is just possible that you did waste those years there. But now you are beginning to ask questions instead of regurgitating what the Professors there have read to you from their lecture notes, it is just possible that there is some hope for you.

"What did they teach you about the Resurrection of the Body anyway? The Nicean Creed? It is just as well that you slept - oh yes, I saw you and I knew why you wore the dark glasses - just as well that you slept through most of those lectures on New Testament theology. And that you were not listening when they tried to prove that all those myths I had placed in the Old Testament were historical fact. Now that you have survived theological school and had a few courses in the School of Hard Knocks, you may be willing to spend a couple of days with Me in the belly of the Big Fish."

"I am glad to learn that You approve because to tell the truth I got more out of those naps than I did from some of the lectures At least I got some much needed rest, and God knows, oh, excuse me. You know that I was stretched pretty tight there trying to go to class, wash cars and change oil at the Gulf Station, and drive out to Owen County to preach on Sundays. And that stint in Indiana. When Paul wrote that he had learned in whatever state he found himself, therein to be content, I knew he had never been in the state of Indiana in the winter time, and not if he aimed to preach what he really believed."

"Now you are getting off the subject and on the verge of bad mouthing the Hoosiers who showed a lot of Christian grace in listening to what you gave them. But there must still be more that you want to know about what I was doing in the Three Days."

I was slow on the uptake, and God went back to the subject of Indiana. "It's a wonder they didn't ride you out of town on a rail the time you lost your temper and dismissed the whole church without even a benediction because a couple of people got up and left while the congregation was singing the invitation hymn."

"You noticed that too, then." I was eager now to change the subject, and I said "Well, this related, distantly maybe, but I always wondered if You played favorites when you are doing all those wonderful things. Not that I could ever suspect You of showing favoritism to me ..."

"Yes, as a matter of fact, I was always partial to the plain Johns and Marys. You will notice that a large part of the New Testament, and in fact, the best of the four Gospels, was written by John, and of course Mary was the chosen one and there was that other Mary whom I was rather attentive to in the Big Story.

"So you could say that I played favorites. I was never impressed by the big name people. Take Pontius Pilate. What an ass. To think, he could wash his hands of Jesus' blood. But Caesar rewarded him properly with lodging in a Roman jail."

"But John. I always wondered if there was just one John who wrote the Gospel and the Apocalypse and those letters too."

"John again. Oh yes, a very common name for some very uncommon men. Well, I was speaking through all of them, but it takes a different John to do the Gospel and one to do the Apocalypse. But then, as I tried to tell you, I created some whole new people capable of doing wonders. And the creation work never stopped. So it could have been. Nothing's impossible."

"Except to get a plain Yes or No answer to a theological question."

"Right. But try to be a little more like Paul on that score too. You are dealing with very big issues here, and I can only give you what your cup will hold. Of course you can always tip it over and pour some of it out on somebody else who is just as hungry and thirsty as you are. That will make room for Me to add some more to your cup.

"Anyway, if you are not entirely satisfied, think on what I've told you for Three Days, and you will be surprised at what you will see when you open your eyes."

CHAPTER TWENTY FIVE

ABOUT JUDAS

"Now what is it?" God sounded as if He had caught me at something I ought not to be doing. Like worshiping an idol. Or contemplating some disaffection. I thought "I am in for a penny, I'll be in for a pound." I said "Judas."

God said "I have heard his name bandied about among the Believers. None of them seem to think very highly of him. What is it you want to know about Judas now?"

I said "Well, why did he do it? And please don't tell me that You planned it for my salvation. I have heard that one until I am sick of it. I want to know the truth. I firmly believe it was his decision, not Yours. I don't believe he was a pawn on Your Chessboard."

"It was his decision, but one he would soon regret."

"I can see that he would soon regret it. But what brought him to do it? Certainly not for the thirty pieces of silver. That's too easy, and it does not do him justice."

"You have read the story in My Book, and you are not satisfied. You still want to know more than is told there?"

"I have read Your Book. I have read the part old Paul wrote to serve as an underpinning for the malarkey that I have heard from Baptist and Methodist pulpits for seventy years. I reckon I could have heard it from the others too if I had been there. Or I could have seen it on the big screen where Mel Gibson has thrown his melodrama of the Crucifixion. But I still have not bought the story because I too have a son, an only son, and I know da... er, very well, that I would not pull a stunt like that on him. Now what I want to know is:

Why did Judas betray Jesus? He knew what was going to happen to him when he was arrested and charged with sedition and heresy and God knows... that is, You know what all else the Jews and the Romans would bring up to stack the deck against Him... Or did he know? Tell me that. Did Judas know what he was doing?"

"I am glad to see you have not asked the question thinking you already have the answer. And the answer is both yes and no."

"Both yes and no? How can that be?"

"Judas knew what he was doing. He did not know the nature or the extent of the consequences of his action. Therefore he did not know what he was doing."

"You have sufficiently confused me. Now will you enlighten me?"

"All Truth is paradoxical. Judas knew and he didn't know."

"So when Jesus prayed Forgive them, for they don't know what they are doing, he was including Judas in His prayer?"

"He could not have left Judas out of that prayer."

"Then what did Judas know? And what didn't he know?"

"He knew that the mission of My Son was not going the way Judas had expected it to go. He did not know the turn events would take when Jesus was arrested."

"Judas didn't know the arrest would lead to Jesus death on the cross?"

"Judas did not, could not know that he himself was starting a conflagration that would sweep over the whole world in a matter of a few hundreds of years."

"You say that Judas knew his expectations were not going to be realized. What did Judas expect to happen?"

"He expected a Macabeean revolt against Rome. A successful revolt attended by divine intervention to set up the Kingdom of Heaven on Earth, with My Son Jesus, as the Davidic Ruler."

"And what made Judas realize that it was not going to be that way?"

"Jesus made him realize it. Jesus spoke very plainly to the effect that He did not intend to raise an armed revolt against Rome."

"And did Judas understand that?"

"Jesus made Judas face the fact that instead of a successful revolt, He was going to become the Scapegoat, the sacrificial Lamb, and Rome would still be in control in Jerusalem, and the Jewish Temple officials would still call the shots in the religious life of the people. But Jesus' goal was very hard for Judas, and the other disciples, to see as a workable plan?"

"And what was Jesus' plan?"

"Not what Satan had offered him in exchange for his worship."

"Then what?"

"To bring true deliverance to the people in their bondage. To truly open the eyes of the blind. To truly enable men to hear what I am saying. To enable them to stand up and walk in dignity before both Me and their fellow men. His Plan was not a military coup, not a political upset. It was to make the poor in spirit, rich in spirit. To lift the fallen to Man's human potential. That was His Dream of the Kingdom of Heaven on Earth."

"And ... ?"

"And Jesus saw very clearly when He confronted the religious leaders in the temple that His Dream of Heaven on Earth was not being accepted by the ruling religious powers, that they did not even believe that was His Goal, did not even see what His Goal was. They saw him as an insurrectionist who was going to upset the apple cart. That is to say, unbalance the balance of power they had struck with Rome. Then Judas saw that was indeed what He was going to do, but without overthrowing the Power of either Judaism or Rome. But Judas did not believe it would work without the overthrow, and he became convinced that Jesus was deluded, and he, Judas, was, going to get him arrested in order to stop the doomed movement. Jesus would be severely castigated by the High Priest, and sent back to Galilee, to do His preaching, His healing, and His befriending of the poor and the underprivileged and the dispossessed there where it would be safe to do those things. He, Judas, would then be Jesus' deliverer. He had got the roles confused and reversed."

"And Judas would go back to Galilee with Him, the treasury enriched by the priests' silver?"

"Possibly. There is no limit to the absurd extremes of the ambitious mind. Certainly he hoped to save the Jesus movement. Then when he saw that he had been deceived by the priests, he threw the money back in his bitterness. He must have felt like the fool that he was. Then he went and hanged himself because he could not face his own gullibility, and he could not face the other disciples who had seen their Master crucified."

"Great God" I said. "The poor devil had no recourse but to hang himself. And his name has become one a man wouldn't give to his dog today."

"Remember," God said. "You asked for it. Nobody else has ever asked me. That's why they have continued to spread the rot they have proclaimed for two thousand years "

"You mean about it being Your Plan of Salvation for sinners like me, and You set Judas up to enable Your Plan to go forward?"

"Right. And I hope you can see the error of your ways by looking at the quality of Jesus' life, and by listening to what He said about the way to live. And I hope you have caught His Dream of the Kingdom of Heaven on Earth for people set free from every form of human bondage. But don't you swallow that tale about being washed clean in His Blood and getting into Heaven free because He paid for your ticket on the Cross?"

I was just about dumbfounded by what I had heard, but being the inquisitive fellow that I am, I said "But Lord, Peter had tried to get Jesus to turn around and go back to Galilee when he realized what was going to happen in Jerusalem."

"True. Peter did try. And got scolded and called Satan for his effort."

"What would have happened if Jesus had done what Peter wanted Him to do?"

"Nothing."

"Nothing?"

"You and I would not even be having this discussion about Jesus of Nazareth and Judas Iscariot."

"You mean ..."

"I mean He would never have been heard of." Then with an ironic twist of humor God said "Oh, Jesus of Nazareth might have become the pastor of the First Baptist Church of Capernaum, or Bethany, or Cana where He would be a welcome guest at all weddings."

"And that's all?"

"That's all."

"Then Your Plan would have been abandoned? It would have been all off."

"Oh no. I never abandon My Ship."

"What then?"

"I would have found a Man for My Purpose."

"Another Man?"

"Man is Man. My Creation. I would not just let My Creation go to hell. What I have made cannot come to nothing. I am God."

CHAPTER TWENTY SIX

ABOUT PETER

"Well Lord," I said, feeling a little more confident about discussing New Testament characters because God had talked so freely with me about Paul. "What about Peter?"

"What about Peter?" God said. "What do you want to know about Peter?"

I wanted to go right to the heart of the matter, so I said "How was it that Peter was the first one of the disciples to recognize Jesus for Who He was? Why did Peter know He was the Christ before anybody else saw it?"

"People see what they are looking for," God explained. "It's as simple as that. Not mysterious at all. Peter was looking for the Christ, and in Jesus he found Him."

"It's still a big mystery for me."

"When three fortuitous events take place together, it is a miracle, whether you want it to be a mystery or not."

"And what are those three events?"

Peter was looking for the Messiah. The Messiah was there. And Peter saw Him."

"That's truly fortuitous all right. But just what did Peter see in Jesus?"

"He saw what John the Baptist had seen. But John had been thrown into prison and he began to question his own judgment because he did not see what he expected happening."

"And You said John had not seen the whole picture. Did Peter see it?"

"Peter was as far off the mark as John was. He was seeing a messiah, but not the Messiah in Jesus' mind. What was shaping up in Jesus' mind was a Messiah Who did not fit Peter's hopes."

"So what did Peter see when he saw the Messiah in Jesus?"

"He saw a Son of David in the Maccabeean image. He saw a Messiah who would liberate His people Israel from the Romans. He didn't realize that Rome was not the tyrant that the Messiah was going to liberate his people from."

"And Peter seems to have persisted in that belief. Otherwise, why would he have that sword tucked under his robe?"

"True. And it took a vision on the Mount of Transfiguration to begin to clarify things for Peter sufficiently for him to even listen to what Jesus was saying about His role as Liberator of Israel."

"I reckon Jesus thought when He and Moses and Elijah were seen together Peter would get the message. But did he see even then what Jesus was about?"

"Peter did not know what to do with that experience. And he still did not make the connection. He still did not see that the Messiah's role was to liberate Israel from the Jewish priesthood who had corrupted true religion."

"Well, but Peter went along with Jesus, and he was all set for the battle. Only he didn't see clearly who the enemy was. But until Jesus started talking about going up to Jerusalem and being killed there."

I was letting what God had said to me soak in, and then I said to Him, "Does all this mean that Peter saw a foretaste of defeat and the collapse of the movement in what Jesus was saying?"

"Yes, and that's why he wanted Jesus to give up the idea of going to Jerusalem. He wanted Him to turn around and go back to Gallilee and strengthen His following until He could be sure of victory. The very thing that is represented in the temptation when Satan offered Him the Kingdoms of the World. But Peter just had not seen what Jesus' idea of the Kingdom was."

"So You are telling me Peter wanted them to turn around and go back to Gallilee? What did Peter hope to accomplish by that? I know You just told me but I still can't see it clearly."

"Gain time. Time for getting a clearer idea of what the revolution was about. Time even to win Jesus over to Peter's idea. And, of course, strengthen the movement. By all means avoid a collision with Rome when the outcome was in doubt. Even strengthen His position vis a vis the religious leaders in Jerusalem before tackling them head on. What Peter did not want to face was the defeat and death which Jesus had spoken of."

"But Peter clung to his dream of conquest right up to the point of Jesus' arrest. He drew his sword and started slashing away with it when the temple police came for Jesus in Gethsemane ... I wonder if Jesus knew Peter had that sword."

"He certainly knew Peter. It was Peter who didn't know Jesus. And when Jesus persisted in His own way, and was arrested, and Peter saw the whole revolution coming to an abrupt end, Peter wanted to disassociate himself from the movement."

"I can understand that. He saw what was happening to Jesus and he didn't want it to happen to him. He wanted to save himself from arrest by Rome. It appeared to him that they had come to the end of the road."

"It was the end of Peter's road."

"And then the resurrection? Is that what turned Peter around so that he could see the right road?"

"That is when Peter turned around. But don't forget what I have been telling you about the resurrection."

"I'm not sure I can even understand what You are saying, even if You repeat it."

"I am saying that Rising From The Dead is what happened to Peter, and to the other disciples of Jesus who had become the Church, His Body on earth. And when Peter finally got the point, saw what was happening, he became invincible. Prison walls could not hold him. The Spirit was free and loose on the earth. Peter had become the Rock that would break down prison doors and set men free in Jesus' Name."

"But Peter still had a problem. Tell me about that Dream at Joppa. What was happening to Peter there?"

"You ought to be able to understand that, after your own experience in Georgia with the racial crisis there."

"Yes, Lord, I reckon I ought to be smarter than I am, and quicker to connect the dots, but it's hard for me to live in two worlds, that one and this one."

I was still wondering about everything, and I said "I am not sure I know what that Dream was about."

God said "I gave Peter a World Vision there. It took a while for him to see it. Peter was a bit slow on the uptake at times. But once he got something, yes, he was like a Rock. Sometimes I find the same problem with you. I have given you two eyes and you still don't see the whole picture clear and true. Even now I have a Petrine task for you to do in the world today. And I will say what Jesus said to Peter: Feed My Sheep. Care for My Little Lambs. Do it with the Word I have given you. See that you write it the way I have spoken it to you."

It seemed to me that God was through with me, but I was not finished with Him because there was something that still bothered me about Peter. So I said "Wait, Lord, according to tradition, Peter was hanged upside down in Rome, and this seems to me to be a humiliating end for a man who had become the Rock and a powerful Voice for the Risen Lord."

"It is," God said. "That's when Peter finally got the message that My Son Jesus came to give him. But don't forget this. It was his victory over Rome."

It took a while for this to soak in, but when it did I could see Peter's identity with his Lord on His Cross where His victory was achieved. Great God. I hope this is not the end of my Conversations with God. I am beginning to look forward to them.

I guess God read my thoughts and put them into words, but as usual He was not going to let me have the last word. He said to me "Now you listen to Me."

CHAPTER TWENTY SEVEN

About Paul the Apostle

"Dear God," I said. "What about this man Paul who calls himself the Apostle to the Gentiles? He was Saul of Tarsus, a leader in the opposition to the Jesus movement. Then there was what every Christian has come to know as The Damascus Road Experience. What happened to him there? Or should I put it differently: What did You do to him that day?"

Then God, Who seemed eager to talk with me about Saul/Paul, or about what He did to him, replied in a manner that made me wonder about my own question: "It was not just what I did to him that day. I had been working on him ever since the Day of Stephen."

"Stephen? What ...?"

"Yes. I put him under the hammer the day they stoned Stephen."

"Oh yes, I remember Saul was assisting at the execution of Stephen."

"You put that well. And I let a few of the stones fall on his conscience."

"You were softening him up then?"

"I let that scene linger in his mind and when I caught him out on the Damascus Road, I, well, to use an expression your brother out in Missouri seems to favor, I knocked Saul of Tarsus on his ass."

"An apt expression, even if my brother in Missouri does favor it. Then what?"

"I hit him with the Big Guns of Heaven."

"The Big Guns of Heaven. Wow."

"I hit him with a thunderbolt. That is, I loosed a bolt of lightning that just blinded him. And a clap of thunder that just about burst his eardrums."

"All of that for one little Jew?"

"All of that for one little Jew who thought he was one big Hebrew, until I hit him."

I said "Wow" again although I know the term is asinine when used in response to God's actions.

He said "but the significance of it is that I made him see and hear."

"Please explain. You are speaking in riddles."

"Not riddles. Paradoxes."

"Then ...?"

"The bolt of lightning that struck him blind opened the eyes of his spirit so that he could see what had been invisible to him before that hit him."

"And..."

"The roll of thunder got his attention so that he could hear My Voice."

"So that's what's meant by that conversation that took place after the lightning strike? But nobody else heard what Paul heard?"

"I wasn't speaking to anybody else. But in the blinding light, Saul saw My Son in the thunder clap he heard His Voice."

"I still don't understand. But maybe if we could come at it another way ... So let me ask You about Paul and Peter. The two main figures in the early Church. They couldn't agree and work together. What was the trouble there?"

"They were not as far apart as you may think. No. They were just too close together there in Jerusalem. And both of them wanted to be Number One. That just can't be. Both of them were very headstrong. Dominant. Not pliable. I had to send Paul out of town to work."

"Well now, Paul once talked as if Peter had things easy, a wife and all the comforts of home while he was storm tossed over the whole Roman world. I guess Peter did have a wife because he had a mother in law. Don't guess Paul envied him that. But there seems to be no romantic attachments in any of Paul's dealings with women. Was he normal?"

"What's normal? For a man with a vision of changing the whole Roman Empire, I would suggest that to tie himself down with a wife and a house full of children, to say nothing of a mother in law inclined to have headaches, that would be abnormal."

"I hadn't thought of all that And a mortgage too, I suppose."

"I hope you are getting the picture."

"I'm trying. But Paul seems at times to just mouth the conventional line about women being submissive to their husbands. I just wondered if he had any experience."

"Lack of experience might have made him more sure of himself on that point."

"And slavery. How could he just close his eyes to the evil of slavery. It would seem that in all those letters he wrote to the churches, he might have included an Emancipation Act that would serve as a model for Lincoln to go by."

"My Man Lincoln didn't need a model. Besides, I had opened Paul's eyes to a larger vision than a civil rights march on the lunch counters or a woman's suffrage crusade. He could overlook those things, or leave them for somebody else. That was not his passion, as people of your day call it. He had a vision, not a dream."

"All right. But what I'm really wondering about is this: his view of sex. He seems to want to lay out the parameters for the man/woman relationship, and to close down all homosexual activities. Did Paul have a real personal problem here.? The reason I ask is that our President has been sounding off and ..."

"Paul did. A lot of men do. His problem was big because he was a big man, even though he bad taken the name Paul to diminish his own ego as the opposite of Saul. But yes, you might say that the preacher was protesting too much in an attempt to deal with his own problem in the area of sex."

"And just what was his problem? It must have been a big one."

"His problem was that he could not accept himself for what he was. So he agonized over the conflict inside himself. Called it his thorn in the flesh, as you doubtless remember. Then he lashed out at the openly practicing homosexuals and sent them packing off to hell. But his real concern was that he himself would be swept along by the tide of his own sexual desires."

"I guess working with those young men, Mark and Timothy and Titus, and Philemon, must have posed some real problems for Paul."

"True. It kept him on the razor's edge of moral anguish over a matter he could do nothing about."

"But what about his view of resurrection? Did he really believe what he was saying on the subject? or was he just up to his eyeballs in something he could not put in words and so he went off into flights of allegories on the subject?"

"He was over his head. But that is not surprising. Nobody has ever comprehended what is meant by that. Everybody tries to explain the unexplainable, and every body winds up in a muddle of words."

"I don't guess You would want to explain it to me in simple language that I could understand."

"Oh I would want to, but I think you would just wind up with another lot of verbiage that would be as confusing as Paul's."

For a moment there God hesitated, and I thought He might be deciding to throw a rare light on the subject, but He didn't so I dashed in with an observation that I thought might stir Him to say something more. "But he claims he saw the Risen Lord."

"And that's what I tried to tell you about striking him blind so that he could see. And deafening him so that he could hear. But obviously it would take a thunderbolt for Me to get through to you in order to reach your understanding of the matter. Yes, Paul saw the Risen Lord Jesus; that was his vision. He heard the Voice of the Risen Lord Jesus; that was his message. Now, you just open your eyes and ears and you will see wonders and hear mysteries that will astound the world.. and even you."

I started to say "I see what You mean." Then I realized that I didn't see, but if I said I did, God would see right through me, so I said "It's been good talking with You about Paul. See you later."

But God had the last word again. He said "It's already later than you think. But keep your eyes and ears open."

Then I realized that was the second time He had said that, and I thought it must be very important, and I did not dare to cause Him to have to say it a third time. So I'm just watching and listening.

CHAPTER TWENTY EIGHT

About the Lost Letters
(A Fiction)

While I was searching for some early church history in Rome I came upon the packet of correspondence about the crucifixion of Jesus in Jerusalem. The letters were tucked into the death notices of some prominent Romans, and the accounts of cost of funerals of these same Romans, all of whom had died in the first century of the Christian era.

There remains a problem of the dating of this material because the Romans did not compute time in terms of the birth of Jesus Christ, but of their own rulers. They were indeed deeply interested in a calendar, but Roman Emperors tended to date events in terms of their own reign because they were more than a little bit egotistical. The one thing we can hang a time cap on though is that all the correspondence between Jerusalem and Rome that was in this packet dates from the death of Jesus, not from his birth.

Caesar Augustus is mentioned in the Book of the Acts of the Apostles, but the term august refers to the character and status of the man bearing it, hence it is a term of great respect and not a proper name. Tiberius was Caesar at the time of Jesus' death. He was the adopted son of the Caesar known as Augustus. Shakespeare said that if we would praise Caesar, we need only to say Caesar, but the dates, by Christian calendar, of the Caesars reigning in the time of this correspondence, are well recorded, and we have mainly to be concerned with Tiberius and Nero, and our main concern is to bring to light the letters which passed between Caesar in Rome and his underlings in Jerusalem who played a crucial role in history because of Jesus Christ.

I was as surprised to find this packet of letters as you are to be reading about them, and I was as skeptical of their authenticity as you are, but the contents convinced me that I had come upon something worth telling. Here it is.

The letters were in Latin, of course, with some Greek thrown in for effect, and that gave me plenty of trouble because it has been a long time since I read Caesar's Gallic Wars, and I have given up reading the New Testament in Greek. But I found help in the person of an old friend, Professor Silas Dinwiddie, retired after many years with the University, and he is an expert in both Latin and Greek. Working with him on the translation, I began to pick up where I had left off many years ago. Still, the translation may be a bit faulty at points. But I am concerned mainly for the sense of what was written in these letters, and I believe it comes through loud and clear. So I bring you here the letters which passed between Jerusalem and Rome on those days and years following the crucifixion of Jesus' of Nazareth.

The first letter was a routine report from Pontius Pilate to Rome. It did not go into detail, certainly not as that event is recorded in the Gospels. It was just a factual account of the arrest, trial, and hanging of the Jew, Jesus ben Joseph, of Nazareth, upon charges brought against him by the Jewish leaders who, Pilate hoped, were pacified, at least temporarily, by the action of the Roman Governor of Judea. Pilate further expressed the hope that the "Pax Romana" would not be disturbed again soon by fanatical messiahs hoping to incite insurrection among the volatile Jews whose major complaint against Rome seemed to be the unpopular tax.

"The Jew, Jesus of Nazareth," wrote Pilate to Caesar, "brought before me and accused of sedition by the Jewish leaders here in Jerusalem. I examined him and found no legal cause for death, would have released him, even offered to exchange him for a known insurrectionist in conformity with a special amnesty agreement, but the Jewish leaders would settle for nothing short of his death."

Pontius Pilate had expected the report to be handled and filed by a department head at the most, but it reached Caesar himself because Pilate had used the term sedition, and because Caesar had given orders that all accounts of death sentences carried out among the, rebellious Jews be brought to his personal attention. He immediately wrote to Pontius Pilate, demanding a complete report, with justification for the crucifixion of a religious figure on a high Jewish religious festival: "You tell me that you have crucified a man whom You examined and in whom you found no cause for death. Do you call that Roman justice? And what have you accomplished for Rome by stirring strong religious prejudices among these people?"

Caesar's letter also informed Pontius Pilate that he already knew about the hanging of Jesus. "News has reached Rome that by hanging this religious leader you have actually created a new religious sect, scattered his followers, and at least two of them have already come to Rome and are forming a group here. They call themselves Followers of the Way, and are active in gaining more followers. They even claim that the crucified prophet Jesus of Nazareth was raised from the dead and lives again. Where is the official record that he was dead when you had him removed from the cross?"

Pontius Pilate was both surprised and frightened. Caesar could remove him from office with a word and have him in a Roman cell with an accusation of misfeasance. Thoroughly shaken, he set about to repair the damages, framing a reply to Caesar with extreme care, both praising Caesar for his concern for justice and justifying his own action as necessary in order to guard Rome against any outbreak of lawlessness in this volatile province inhabited by a race of people difficult to govern because of their fanatical religious superstitions.

Pilate wrote "The man Jesus, a Jewish rabbi and prophet from Galilee had become a threat to the peace and security of the province here and a possible threat to Rome, even to you, noble Caesar. He led a rowdy crowd of his followers into Jerusalem, acting out the religious symbolism and political hopes going back to the early times when the Jews exercised power in the region under a king called David. The people following him embodied the hope that he might establish that power again, a feat he could only accomplish by overthrowing the power of Rome.

"He further challenged both the Jewish religious leadership and Rome with inflammatory statements about the temple which is the center of the Jewish worship here, saying that if Rome threw it down he would rebuild it in three days. This is clearly an assertion of power that is greater than the power of Rome itself And when asked about paying the Roman taxes he gave a cryptic answer about rendering to Caesar what is Caesar's, while we know that taxation in fact is a matter of Caesar taking what they claim to be theirs, and he also gave some cryptic response about finding the tax money in the mouth of a fish.

"This was an account which my intelligence gatherers had come upon in talking with some of his followers and was at first suspect of being nothing more than the lore that accumulates around religious heroes. Some of his most ardent followers are known to be professional fishermen, and it is possible that at times they rise to professional status in telling fish tales, one of which involves a miraculous haul of fishes under his direction that even put their boat in peril of being capsized because of the weight of the fishes.

"At first I believed him to be a harmless religious fanatic credited with doing miracles of healing and other more spectacular things, even walking on water. But as the trial went on, it became evident to me that that he had political aims camouflaged by religious language. He talked about the Kingdom of Heaven which he had come to usher in on the earth, but he was never clear about the effects of this Kingdom of Heaven on the Empire of Rome.

"All of this may seem like harmless blather until one gathers a crowd of yelling, chanting followers, and begins to act out symbolic roles that raise the enthusiasm of followers to violence, ergo, invading the temple of the Jews and driving the Jewish authorities out.

"You know, noble Caesar, that we have always tried to keep things peaceful here by letting the Jewish leaders have their religion so long as it does not interfere with law and order or challenge the supremacy of divine Caesar. But for a brigand from the hills to ride in and challenge established religious leaders is an act of terror."

Since Jesus' own disciples seemed at times unable to comprehend what he meant by the Kingdom of Heaven or of God, it is not surprising that the Roman Governor attached a political rather than a spiritual meaning to it.

This second letter of the Governor to Caesar, instead of spreading oil on the troubled water, evoked sharp criticism from Caesar who was unfavorably impressed by Pontius Pilate's attempt to justify himself after the fact when his first report had indicated that he had not found any crime in Jesus and had merely given way to the Jews who were determined to have a human sacrifice at their high, holy season of the Passover.

Caesar wrote to Pontius Pilate: "It now appears to me that instead of suppressing religious fanaticism among the Jews you have helped to create a new and more virulent religion that not only divides the Jews into warring camps, but is threatening to create trouble here in Rome. Already my spies inform me that there are the Peter versus Paul factions within the Jewish religion, and both of them are working to bring about dissatisfaction with Roman customs of offering worship to the divinity of Caesar, and thereby weakening the authority of Rome."

Caesar now launched into a matter of theological and political importance to Rome. "You know what the reason for declaring the divinity of Caesar was: to establish the supremacy of Rome in all matters and eliminate those competing religions that functioned as a divisive force in the lives of the people. You also know that the weakness of the divinity of Caesar inheres in the fact that even divine Caesar is mortal;

he must die. Now you have launched upon the empire a new divinity who actually overcomes death, is raised from the dead and lives again. And is expected to return as the all powerful conqueror of Rome."

Caesar's candor in revealing the weakness or flaw in the official religion of Rome is surprising, and can only be explained by the fear which the Resurrection which the Christians claimed for their Lord Jesus had struck in him. It also raises the question whether Caesar himself really believed in the divinity myth which had been fabricated to strengthen the Empire, and whether he realized that it only made him more vulnerable than his humanity did.

The emergence of Christianity as a political and religious force had shaken Caesar, but Pontius Pilate's reply to Caesar is of great interest because it is very defensive, and shows that be had done thorough research into the Jesus movement, and wanted Caesar to believe that far from failing to serve Rome's interests, he had in fact preemptively, acted to protect Rome from a real and growing threat. "Divine Caesar, this miracle worker whom the populace had begun to call Messiah and Son of God, and who called himself Son of Man, no doubt to establish his base with the common people, had already begun to gain followers among Romans here who were influenced by his healing powers. One Roman Centurion had even sought his help in the matter of healing a servant of his, and this had caused such a stir that I had the Centurion demoted, and I feel that far from causing trouble over this Jesus incident, I have suppressed an uprising, the extent and intensity of which can only be comprehended if we remember the Maccabeean era and what eventually happened at the tragic rock which has become a holy shrine to all Jews who still harbor the dream of independence and world power."

Venturing now upon the uncertain seas of political ambition, Pontius Pilate claimed that far from deserving the rebuke from Caesar, he merited reward and promotion. Easing into the area of consolidation of power in himself, Pontius Pilate pointed out that "Most of the trouble with religious fanatics and extremists originates in Galilee, far from central control in Jerusalem and in Samaria where a mixed breed of people are ready for any change in government. If both

Galilee and Samaria were brought under one central power here it would serve the purpose of Rome." He stopped short of saying that he hoped to be that Central Power, but he left no room for doubt about his intention.

Caesar, averse to the consolidation of power in anybody's hands other than his own, studied this last suggestion closely, and decided that Pontius Pilate himself would be a fit subject for study, to determine not only his loyalty to the divine Caesar, but his sanity in dealing with Jewish Messianism.

Then Caesar remembered Judas Iscariot, and he wanted to know more about his role, in the drama of the Risen Christ, so he decided to conceal his doubts about Pontius Pilate until he had learned more from him about this man who was credited with having turned Jesus over to the authorities. so he asked, and by inquiring into the role of Judas, Caesar unwittingly gave Pontius Pilate a new opportunity to put himself forward as the savior of the Empire. For Pontius Pilate came back and represented Judas as a plant in the original band of followers of Jesus. He also launched an attack on the more militant members of that band of followers.

"Judas was rather easily bought off," wrote Pontius Pilate. He was already the treasurer for the group of disciples, and it took only thirty pieces of silver. Others though were dangerous men. Simon, nicknamed Peter, a violent man, ready to take up arms to protect Jesus from the Jews but he hid his sword quickly enough when Roman soldiers appeared. He has now a following in Jerusalem and possibly even in Rome. James and John, the brothers who Jesus called "sons of thunder", have been dealt with harshly. I put James to death, but John escaped and I understand is active writing. We will see whether the pen is mightier than the sword.

"It is easy for them to flee beyond the limited borders of my jurisdiction though ... then carry on their seditious activity by writing things that keep the memory Of Jesus alive, and foster the worship of him as the divine Son of God. It is my hope, Great Caesar, that you will see that I, while acting with caution and patience in dealing with this Jewish Messiah, have in fact done away with the head of the movement, for no sane person could believe the women's tale about a resurrection from the dead.

"Jesus of Nazareth is dead and will stay dead."

But great power had produced a paranoia in Caesar. He could not put aside the story of Jesus' resurrection as women's tale, and he was offended by Pilate's words because he had begun to take the story seriously, but neither could he speak freely and openly about his fears lest the Senate and the Army become suspicious that he was entertaining a dangerously foolish belief in Jesus himself. Yet he needed to talk with someone, and he thought long and hard about WHO that Someone might be. Someone level headed and loyal and with no ambition for power. But who could that be? Everybody in Rome was ambitious for power.

Then Caesar recalled the name of an old retired general, Carollus Tertullus, who lived on a farm about twelve miles from the city of Rome. Yes, he would visit and talk with the old general. But he would have to be careful what he said to him, for no man can be trusted with one's deepest fears; it gives him even a power over the one who confesses his fears.

Tertullus, seventy two years old, still ramrod straight and with a Roman Eagle of a nose that could smell out trouble even at a distance was a veteran of the wars that had brought Palestine under Roman control. He would be both experienced in matters dealing with the Jews, and too old to be a threat to the young Caesar's own power. So it was to Tertullus that Caesar went with the double bladed question of what was to be done about the spread of Christianity in the Empire, and the ambition, indeed the level headedness, even the sanity, therefore the fitness for office, of Pontius Pilate.

"But what about his followers?"

Tertullus' reply: "Now that is a harder question to answer because they don't all see him the same way. I am told that one of them, Simon, the one they call Peter because he is the Rock of the group, actually attacked one of the arresting officers. Others have been less inclined to sword play. None of them has dared to raise a sword against a Roman soldier. My sources of information tell me that they have scattered, and this makes it more difficult to keep up with all their movements. But I believe they are limited mostly to preaching. What is disturbing to me is that they claim that Jesus is still alive. I should say alive again. And that he has even been seen by some of them and has spoken to them since he came back to life."

"So what about Pontius Pilate's story that he has saved the Roman Empire from a bloody revolution by putting the fellow to death? Did he exaggerate in order to justify his action? Did he panic, and then try to rationalize his action? Or is it all a political ploy on Pilate's part to gain a larger measure of rule for himself?"

Tertullus' reply: "It's hard to say, noble Caesar. Maybe none of the above. Maybe Pontius Pilate really tried to get Jesus off the hook, and neither Jesus nor the Jews would let him, and now he wants to cover his own weakness in dealing with a situation that was more than he could handle. My judgment is that the Jews needed a sacrifice for the Passover, and Jesus was willing to be, even determined to be that sacrifice. The Jews are a very complicated people, and the things they will do in their obsession with their religion are difficult for the Roman mind to comprehend."

"Then you are saying that Pontius Pilate got caught in a box and couldn't figure his way out of it?"

Tertullus: "That's entirely possible The Jews are master box builders."

"But Roman rulers are required to be masters of men, even of men who are master box builders."

Tertullus: "as you say, divine Caesar. Roman rulers have to be more than common men. They have to be gods."

The old Roman soldier's account of this visit does not vary greatly from Caesar's but in certain particulars, it was essentially a different version of what transpired between them. Tertullus wrote: "Caesar seemed to be deeply concerned about the myth that Jesus of Nazareth had risen from the dead, and he even seemed to have given credence to the possibility that the myth of the Virgin Birth was more than a myth but possibly a supernatural event, and between the two events Virgin Birth and Resurrection any miracle could be believed. He really seemed to be in danger of becoming a Christian. He seems to have been influenced by Greek mythology in this respect, and it maybe that infusion of our Roman system of education with Greek teachers has produced this effect."

There were many writers within the Christian community, and they were giving concern to both Caesar and his underlings. Numerous accounts of the life, death and resurrection of Jesus were written, with accounts of his teachings. It seems that every Christian had a story to tell, and told it, in writing, as well as in speaking, and the story of the resurrection was the one to catch the ear.

These stories about Jesus floated about everywhere, and they influenced people in high and low estate. But there is a long gap in the correspondence with Rome: The infamous Nero was Caesar, and the two writers' who wielded the most power were Paul and John. But the correspondence that catches our eye is that between Caesar and Agrippa; the subject is Paul. The history of Paul's conversion to Christianity, his missionary efforts in the Mediterranean world, and his conflict with the Jews, have been chronicled in The Acts, and it is just this conflict with the Jews that brought him to the attention of Caesar and produced the letters between Jerusalem and Rome concerning him.

Pontius Pilate is history; he has been called to Rome to face judgement there, and we may assume that Caesar, at that time Tiberius, has dealt with him but there is no account of how he did it in the letters which I found. The new and disturbing star in the heavens over the Roman world is the little Jew Paul, who is causing such a disturbance among the Jews that he comes into contact with Roman officials. Paul was brought first before Felix at Caesarea and Felix was unable to resolve the issue; he brought Paul to Festus who was coming to take his place apparently; Festus found it too perplexing and the two, Felix and Festus, brought Paul before King Agrippa, and it was Agrippa who wrote the account to Caesar and then sent Paul on to Rome. Agrippa himself seemed to be teetering on the brink, but let us see his own account to Caesar which is very carefully worded.

"Noble Caesar, Felix and Festus, the Jews provoking them, brought this Jew, Paul, formerly known as Saul of Tarsus, before me. He was charged with Offense against the Law of the Jews, but what concerns Rome is that he was charged with proclaiming a King of Heaven greater than Caesar, and he made no denial of it.

"In fact, he based his claim of Jesus' greatness on the story that he had risen from the dead. And he certainly knew where to touch the sore spot. Rome's ultimate power lies in the ability to put men to death. Well, if a criminal can come back from death and reassert his life and influence, then he claims a power that exceeds the power of Rome, and a dignity exceeding that of Great Caesar. Now this fellow I am sending to you is somebody special because he claims to be a Roman citizen, by birth, and he wants his case brought to you. He seems to think he can jump over all the intermediaries and appeal directly to Caesar. I assume he may challenge you with this new divinity, the Risen King of Heaven.

Caesar now Nero occupies that role acknowledged Agrippa's report but replied in words that let Agrippa know that had already heard the rumor of Agrippa's near conversion under the persuasive words of Paul. "And you," Caesar answered, "Have you become a believer in this Risen One?"

Caesar was in no hurry to see Paul. It is just as well, for Paul's sea journey was slow and perilous, but he eventually reached Rome, was put under house arrest, and reports went regularly to Caesar of his activities. Paul occupied himself with writing letters of guidance and encouragement to the churches. Many of these letters were preserved; some probably have been lost. None was found in the Packet under discussion here. But, there was a letter from Caesar to King Agrippa regarding his unusual prisoner, Paul.

"Caesar, in Rome, to Agrippa, King in the land of the Jews: You have sent me this troublesome preacher to disturb my dreams at night, and I would put him in the arena with the lions, but I value the lions and I fear that he would so fill their mouths with his preaching of Jesus Christ that they would choke on his words."

Peter also had made his way to Rome and was having measurable success in his proclamation of the Gospel, apparently having overcome the fear that Possessed him on the night of Jesus' arrest, but not having reached accord with Paul on the relationship of the Gospel of Jesus and the law of Moses. Caesar commented on this in his letter to Agrippa: "I have Peter here too and have decided that the only way to settle the controversy between him and Paul is to behead both of them. Your own head will not rest easy if you repeat the act of sending pesky Jews to me when I have the weight of the Empire on my shoulders and the fires that consume a great part of the city itself. Remember Pontius Pilate, and profit from his Mistakes."

Pilate had been recalled to Rome and severely disciplined for bungling the matter of the death of Jesus. It is uncertain from the documents in the packet just how Pilate was disciplined, whether imprisoned or put to death. Certainly his ambitions had not served him well with the Caesar on the throne at the time of the death of Jesus.

Even while Paul was on his way to Rome, another writer in Rome itself, was giving Caesar cause for both wonder and concern. He was known as John, possibly a pen name, for many Christian documents appeared under that name. Legend has it that this John was a prisoner on the Isle of Patmos at the time of writing. He claims that he had received a revelation from God and he had written a most inflammatory document that had come to be known as the Apocalypse. It has become a part of the canonical New Testament and is known to the whole Christian world. Caesar's comment on the Apocalypse was terse, but it reveals the grave concern it gave him. "I cannot understand it. It seems to be written by one madman for consumption by other madman, but certainly no good can come of it for Rome."

Completely out of place chronologically in the packet of materials I found the reference to Herod's dealing with some of the inner circle of disciples of Jesus. Tiberius was Caesar at the time and it was to him that Herod had sent the report that he had executed James, one of the Sons of Thunder, and had arrested Peter, but a strange thing happened. Herod wrote to Caesar: "The guards brought this cock and bull story about an angel coming in the night and rescuing Peter right out of their hands, and so this Prince of the Apostles escaped, but I had the guards executed. There is no limit to the superstitions of the Jews and they even corrupt Roman soldiers with their beliefs in angels and divine interference.

Caesar had written a terse reply to King Herod: "Arrest the angels and get medical assessment for any guards assigned to these prisoners in the future."

This did not solve any problems for Rome. Caesar Nero was still having to deal with Peter, while that Apocalypse of John was circulating among the churches, and Paul was on his way to Rome because Felix and Festus and Agrippa had all fumbled the ball with him. Paul was destined to become the most influential of Christian writers, doing it from a Roman prison, and the reason is that he had seized upon the one thing that neither the Jews nor the Romans could counter, the Resurrection of Jesus Christ. It was this one point that made Jesus superior to the Law of Moses. It was what baffled Felix and Festus and Agrippa, and when he told about his own experience on the Damascus Road when the Risen Lord struck him down with a bolt of lightning, blinding and opening his eyes at once, that he convinced his judges of his madness, but growing impatient with both the obtuseness of the Jews and the inability of the Roman governors to understand what he was talking about, he had appealed directly to Caesar, and to Caesar he was sent. It was a Caesar not likely to be friendly, but the die was cast.

So the final report to Rome, signed by both Festus and Agrippa, had indeed presented a real problem to Caesar in the person of Paul. "Divine Caesar," the letter began, "this man Paul, the troublesome preacher of a Risen Christ, the same being one Jesus of Nazareth, crucified, by edict of Pontius Pilate in an attempt to assuage the anger of the Jews, thus Paul is the most ardent advocate of Jesus. He also speaks of a Holy Ghost, some invisible power that inhabits the followers of Jesus, and he further maintains that this Risen One will return to rule the world. This rule he calls the Kingdom of Heaven. All of this is a puzzle too great for us here in Jerusalem, and the man Paul being a Roman citizen, and requesting your judgment, we are sending him to you."

As I have already indicated, Caesar was not happy to have this bothersome problem dumped into his lap by what he had already come to consider bumbling politicians eager for more power than they were capable of handling with wisdom. Yet he was also attracted to it because of the element of mystery surrounding the crucified Messiah who, according to his followers, was risen from the dead and preparing for an imminent return in overwhelming power. Caesar's second letter to Agrippa was sarcastic: "so you are sending me the Jew Paul who claims to have seen the Risen Christ. Perhaps he will tell me what he looks like and what is his time of return. Are you sending the Holy Ghost too to prepare me to understand these mysteries?

"Well, I will get it straight from the Jew's own mouth. He may even be able to throw some light on the Apocalypse written by the fellow calling himself John and disturbing Rome with his dreams and visions. One madman to interpret another. Now I suspect that not only are the Christians mad, but they have infected Roman officials in Jerusalem with their madness."

Softening somewhat, for even Nero had a small soft streak, Caesar's letter continued: "Peter, who is said to be the Rock on which the church is built, has not been helpful at all to me in my attempt to understand the mysteries. I wonder if he does. He is indeed as solid as a rock in his loyalty to Jesus, but it is a pity he was not enlisted in the Roman army. He would have made a crack centurion if not a chief captain. Keep the lid on tight in Jerusalem, or we my have to destroy that temple there and test whether their risen Christ can rebuild it in three days."

Agrippa did not draw much comfort from Caesar's letter, but he was relieved to have Paul off his hands and on his stormy way to Rome. The storms at sea which made the journey perilous for Paul did not bother Agrippa much. He remarked to Felix and Festus that if Paul had not asked to be sent to Rome he might have been released. But a note from Felix to Agrippa indicated that "the Jew's life would not be worth a plugged denarius if he were turned loose among his countrymen. Remember the forty hungry Jews who took the oath. I wouldn't want even Paul to fall into their hands here."

Upon receiving notice that Paul had arrived in Rome, alive and ready to preach to the Romans, Caesar sent one more note to Agrippa: "So you three can't handle one little old Jew. Paul is here now, after a perilous voyage by sea which has put the lives of Roman sailors at risk. His Risen Jesus, who is reputed to have controlled the waves on the Sea of Galilee has brought him through the storms of the Mediterranean. Now I must try to make sense of the trumped up charges against him. Meanwhile, he is converting Rome to Christianity. He works on every guard assigned to him and is so persuasive I expect the whole Praetorian Guard to go over to his Risen Christ. How long before the Cross replaces the Roman Eagle on our battle flag?"

The correspondence ended with this prophetic question. The Romans did destroy the Jewish Temple in Jerusalem about the middle of that first century that is dated by the birth of Christ, and the Cross did fly in the Roman Banner less than three hundred years later when the Emperor Constantine waged war to extend the power of Rome, and of the Risen Christ.

CHAPTER TWENTY NINE

ABOUT HARLOTS & FALLEN WOMEN

"It's about harlots, Lord ... and fallen women," I said. "I was wondering ..."

"Always wondering," God said, but He didn't seem displeased with me about wondering. In FACT, He seemed amused. Maybe it was the subject matter of my wondering that amused Him. "What is it you are wondering about harlots and fallen women?"

"Well, they keep cropping up in Your Book. And in the most peculiar manner too. But the way people talk about them, well, I was wondering if maybe You have a different take on the subject."

"A different take! Now you begin to talk like somebody doing an interview on a popular talk show. Speak English, if you can't speak Hebrew or Greek or Latin."

"Well, what I want to say is that I was taught that these women were bad and ought to be avoided. I remember we had a Red Light District for them and decent people just... and I assumed that You had assigned them to perdition. And then I read in Your Book about Rahab."

"Of course. Rahab. She was the woman who saved my two good men trapped in Jericho. Hid them from their pursuers and then let them down by a cord over the wall, and they escaped."

"That was a smart trick of deceit all right. Comparable to the wooden horse the Greeks used to get inside the city of Troy. But to tell the truth, I was wondering what those two Hebrew spies were doing in her house of ill repute. I would not expect them to put up at the Jericho Arms. But wasn't there a respectable place in town. There they could stay while they were spying out the place and getting an idea of its defenses and weak spots?"

"Respectable place! Don't you realize that any good citizen of Jericho would have turned them in to the authorities and they would have been hanging from the wall? That would have ended their career as spies and aborted the planned invasion."

"The invasion. Yes, Lord, about the invasion. I have always had some questions about the ethics of the way the Hebrew people came in and took over the Land of Canaan. But I still wonder why those two men were in Rahab's house and just what …"

"It was a safe place. The only safe place in town. And in exchange for saving my men from the people, the hunting party intent on killing them, Rahab and her family were saved when the Hebrew people took the town."

"And the scarlet thread. That's always been a romantic element of the story."

"Yes, the scarlet thread became the sign that marked, identified Rahab's house and saved her whole family when the Hebrew people took the town. Too bad it has become a symbol of shame and disgrace. But yes, Rahab, saved my two men and the scarlet thread saved Rahab."

"Well, I reckon it is a long jump from Joshua's time to that of Jesus, even though, the name seems to be the same, but I notice that Jesus showed partiality to the harlots too. Said they would be given preference at the gate of heaven over the highly respected religious leaders of His day."

"My son rightly discerned human character. But the leap of time you mention appears to you to be a great one, while it is a part of completing the picture for Me. An eye blink and another touch of the brush on the canvas. The important thing is that My Son offered them salvation. The harlots accepted what the religious leaders rejected. He offered the Kingdom of Heaven, and the harlots eagerly rushed in while the scribes and the Pharisees and the Sadducees organized a hunting party to take His Head."

"Well, I always wondered about the woman at the well in Samaria, and the one who was about to be stoned because she had been caught in the act of adultery."

"And well you might wonder about both of these women. My Son showed both mercy and understanding to those women, but His enemies, the established religious leaders, were concerned with upholding their standards, not saving the people who fell short of their standards."

"Hmmm. Sounds a lot like people today. Well, just what is it all about? Why are fallen women given preference, even the only place, while the leaders of society are consigned to perdition, even death?"

"The women are honest."

"But I thought an honest woman was one who ..."

"... has an honest product to sell. You get what you pay for, and not a fleecing."

"Well, what became of those women? The Samaritan woman. Now she seems to be willing to settle for crumbs. Did she get the crumbs? And the woman rescued from the would be stoners. He told her to go and sin no more. But go where? Could she go back home to her husband? Go back to church and the women's class there? Go join the Garden Club? Where did she go, to sin no more?"

"Where indeed?! They went to gather palm branches to wave before Him when He rode into Jerusalem. They went to anoint His Head and His Feet for the burial. They went to weep at the foot of the cross. They went to stand amazed at an empty tomb. They went to assure Peter and the other big strong men that all was not lost. They entered the Kingdom of Heaven. They offered their bodies and became members of the Body, the Glorious Church that arose on Easter Day."

"Gee, thanks Lord. I never realized …"

"Don't bother to thank Me. Just Go and write the things I have told you. And do it now, before you forget. Go write My Words."

CHAPTER THIRTY

About David

I was thinking about the most famous man in the Old Testament when I became aware of God's Presence, and I turned to Him and said "Well Lord, this time it's about David. King David," I added and immediately realized that it was silly to make this clarification for God already knew. I guess it was because I felt that God might be sensitive about David, because David was a very special man with God. So I said "But I don't know just where to start." Then God let me know where to start.

"Why not start at the beginning? That's the proper place to begin. What do you want to know about David?"

I said "Well, I thought we might talk some about him. The first thing I remember from Sunday School when I was just a little boy is the story about David and Goliath. Now I wonder, Did David really kill the giant with a little stone from the brook? Or is that just the sort of tale that legends are made of after a hero becomes a national figure, a real hero?"

"Why would you doubt that David felled the giant with a stone from his sling? That was the most effective weapon to use from a safe distance. You don't think that boy was going to walk into the giant's arms to try to match his brute strength, do you? That would have been suicide."

I had not thought about it that way, and I said "I thought maybe a slingshot was just for shooting sparrows," but immediately I saw I had said the wrong thing, for God informed me that He is already on record in His Book about His feelings about the falling of sparrows. So I tried to change the subject to get on safer ground. I said "I reckon old Goliath was not a mental giant."

God said "He was not, but his defeat brought David to the attention of Saul. And that was critical."

"Yes Lord, and I was just wondering about that. I realize that young David was a mighty warrior, but I get the idea that it was being taken into Saul's family that gave him his real boost, and I was wondering if..."

"Always wondering," God said, but He did not seem displeased by my wondering. So I said "It seems to me that David might have used his place in the family of Saul to undercut the authority of the King and to erode the King's self confidence, and eventually to steal his crown." After I said this I wondered if I had said too much, but God let me go on with this line of reasoning. I said "David and Jonathan were great friends, and Jonathan who is the natural heir to the throne does not even seem to be aware that David is the brown headed cow bird who is going to steal that throne right out from under him."

"Your mixture of metaphors still gets the idea across," God said. "But Jonathan didn't want the crown. He had seen what it did to his father's head, and he was not eager to try to fit it to his own head. And he could see that David was the one more fitted to the crown and the throne. But you have other things you are wondering about too, so out with them."

"Well yes, Lord. There is Michal, Saul's daughter. David married her, but they didn't hit it off very well. Sort of blows the romantic idea of marriages made in heaven."

"Marriages are made on Earth. If the marriage is good, then marriage is heaven. If it's bad, the marriage is hell. But Michal was not the woman for David. She interfered with David's worship of Me."

"You mean she tried to …?"

"I mean she attempted to interpose her idea of royal dignity between David and the free and spontaneous expression of his devotion to Me. Tried to make it appear scandalous for David to dance naked in his expression of joy and adoration in the realization of My approval of him."

"And a rather nasty domestic scene ensued, I guess from the account in Your Book."

"Yes, and David sent her to the broom closet, so to speak, and her father Saul gave her to another man, Phalti the son of Laish. You would never have heard of Phalti the son of Laish if he had not been the second choice for Michal, but the world would hear of David plenty after Michal was gone from his bed."

"Yes Lord, but I notice that David had several adventures with women. He did not sleep alone just because the King's Daughter was no longer in his bed."

God seemed to be waiting for me to say more, and I said "There was Abigail."

"Yes. What is your question about Abigail?"

"Well, Abigail was a married woman. Maybe not a happily married woman, but … well, I guess she wouldn't be happy if she was married to a churlish fellow like Nabal. Still …"

"You don't seem to be able to frame your question, so I will do it for you. Yes, Nabal was unwilling to pay the price of freedom, but Abigail saw David as the Liberator; she paid the price willingly; Nabal paid the price of his own villainy. He paid with his life."

"And David got his wife Abigail and the whole storehouse of goods that Nabal was trying to guard and keep for himself, but …"

"But what?"

"But David looks like a Mafia boss. He is collecting protection money. And he exacts a terrible price from anyone who does not pay willingly for his protection "

"The duty of the ruler is to protect his people; the right of the ruler is to tax the people in payment for their protection."

"But David was not yet King. Saul was still …"

"David was My Chosen, My Anointed. He was doing what Saul had proved he was unable to do. He was protecting My People from their enemies."

I was trying to stick to my position, and doing it by repeating it. "So David got Abigail and the storehouse too. But his adventure with Bathsheba was a scandal. Surely You did not approve of what he did there."

"I did not approve. And David soon knew that I did not approve "

"He knew? And still …?"

"I sent My Prophet Nathan to tell him a story that you way wish you had Written. And when David found himself in the net of Nathan's weaving, he knew."

"So was what he did with Bathsheba worse than what he did with Abigail?"

"Much worse."

"How? In both cases he took another man's wife and the man wound up dead."

"Bathsheba's husband was a soldier in David's army. He was fighting to support David's throne. When David killed him he kicked a leg from under his own throne. So he weakened the throne and imperilled My People. So he had sinned against My People and had thrown a stumbling block in the way of My Purpose for Israel. That was an intolerable act, and it could not go unpunished."

"I guess he felt the lash when that baby died. But yet he was described as a man after your own heart. How could that be when he had done the things he had done? I have even heard men say David was the prototype of Christ Himself."

"David was devoted to me. That was always My first requirement. That's why it is My First Commandment. He did some things I did not approve. But he was worth punishing, for he learned under the lash of his punishment. He suffered, and he repented, and I forgave him. But that does not mean that he would have smooth sailing into a safe port. No. His own sons gave him enough trouble to make him know that he was paying for the deeds he had done."

"Yes, Lord. David must have thought he had spawned a nest of copperheads. What, possessed those sons to make them try to dethrone their own father and seize the power they didn't know how to handle."

"Their not knowing was what drove them, together with their greed for power."

"Why couldn't they wait for the King to die?"

"Because of Solomon."

"Solomon? How?"

"They knew that. Solomon was chosen to be King, and they tried to get ahead of him."

"Why was Solomon chosen?"

"He was wise."

"Wiser than any of his brothers?"

"Wiser than all of them."

I decided to try to switch the conversation to David's contribution to literature and music. I asked "Did David write all those Psalms? Or was that a collection attributed to him because he was the Great King and this would give more authority to the work?"

"Did you ever know of any great work of art or music or literature put together by a committee? David was a genius. You should hope to write something that would make men ask whether you really wrote it."

"The Twenty Third is the people's favorite. Is it Yours?"

"That one is perfect. You should try to match it."

"I might shoot at it, but my arrow would fall to the ground short of its goal. I guess nobody else ever hit it either." But God seemed to be waiting for me to ask a relevant question instead of just saying the obvious, and I said "I reckon you were not offended when Your Son Jesus was hailed as the Son of David?"

"My Son Jesus was indeed the son of David. And the son of Solomon. He was what David aspired to be in Power, and what Solomon was in Wisdom. This Father/Son relationship is the True Mystery of My Creation. You would do well to learn of this and alter your course accordingly."

God is always bringing it back to me, but I did not see just what He was getting at and I stood with my mouth open. He said "One day you may be able to get it right."

I was still uncertain of the ground I was standing on but I was sure it was holy ground. Still, I had one more question, and even though it seemed that God was dismissing me, I went right ahead and asked when He gave me the sign to speak again. "It's about Abishag," I said. "The girl they brought to David when he seemed to be failing fast and they wondered whether his head would hold up the crown ..."

"Yes. What is it you want to know about Abishag?"

"Well, Lord, that's my question to You. What was it about Abishag? It seems that the King and all the King's sons wanted Abishag."

"You would have had to know Abishag to understand. She was truly My Creation as a Gift for the King."

CHAPTER THIRTY ONE

The Creation Myth and the Rise of Man

It is my opinion that the stories in the early chapters of Genesis have been misread as the Fall of Man. I believe we have here an account of the Rise of man from the innocence of childhood to the full stature of mature and responsible manhood. This Rise, like the actual experience of growing up, involves a struggle between the child and the father.

In the Creation Myth, Man is trying to become like God, and God is fighting back to keep that place of privileged Power from falling into the hands of Man. In the Creation Myth, Man is made in the image and likeness of God. But God has made a two headed bundle of trouble for Himself because this little image Man - male and female - will insist on growing up into a real Man who will challenge God for that place of creative Power that he recognizes to be the very essence of Deity.

So the serpent was right about the effect of eating the fruit of the Tree of Knowledge of Good and Evil, and the reaction of God to Man's intrusion on His special territory. This is not the story of a Fall into Original Sin; it is the myth about the eternal struggle of Man upward to a place beside God Himself, and of God's resistance to Man's effrontery in wanting that position. But first, what is a Myth?

Myth is a picturesque way of presenting a Truth that is too big for the language of fact, and will not fit into the mold of scientifically accurate journalism.

Myth depicts a meeting of God and Man on the plane of history. And God, being of Godly proportions, and Man, aspiring to those same dimensions, it becomes necessary for the story teller to resort to a certain type of language, the language of Myth, designed to both instruct and entertain, at the same time. Instruction, by its very nature unpalatable to egoistic Man, is made palatable by being presented in the form of entertainment. The myths attempt to do this in dealing with the philosophical questions which present themselves to the mind of man in every culture. The Biblical Myth of Creation, found in Genesis One and Two, does this in noble language superior to that of most of the world's creation myths. But it is not different in essence from them: God made man, using Himself as the pattern, and the action begins.

So to say that the creation story is myth is not to say that it is not true. It is to say that it is A TRUTH that requires no proof, cannot be proved nor disproved. God created Man in His own image and there is no other explanation for the Godlikeness of Man. Nor is there an explanation for God, other than what Man sees God to be.

But to be made in God's image and likeness has to mean something; it means that Man has Power, or at least aspires to Power, to have dominion or aspires to dominion, over the whole world, because our earliest concept of God is of Power and Dominion over the Created World.

Every group of people, whether they are literate like the Athenians, or illiterate like some African jungle tribe, has a creation myth. This is because people everywhere and at all times, have needed an answer to the question: How did I get here in this wonderful and dangerous world? And the answer in the opening words of the Book of Genesis, is a good one. It may be the best one yet. But it is not a factual account of creation. Instead, it is a religious story, the account of man's first encounter with God; it is a superb myth.

Because we have no eye witness account of creation, it was necessary to create a myth of creation. And lacking any other causal factor, the myth maker must fall back on God, which means that the conclusions cannot be demonstrated by scientific methods, so the old question of Creation versus Evolution is irrelevant to this discussion. We have a myth which deals with ultimate Truth rather than day to day events that may require millions of years for the scientist. So, while myth is not fact, it is Truth. And the Truth is to be seen in the nature of the myth itself. God creates the world, makes Man whom He puts in the world, delegates Power to that Man, but of course God wants to keep something for Himself alone.

And of course what God wants to keep for Himself would be the very thing that Man would want. And because this secret that God is keeping must be the secret to God's own being, and consequently the secret to Man's own being and destiny, the Creation Myth is first rate entertainment and bound to be instructive.

And the secret? It is Knowledge, the ability to discern between Good and Evil.

For at this point Man is a Babe who has not even seen himself. Has only looked up into his Father's Face, and, in wonder, has begun to dream of what he himself might be. He does not even know at this point that he is himself the mirror image of what he is seeing up above him. He may suspect it, but he must find out for himself, and the only way he can find out is to test the One up there. He can test Him by exploring the boundaries.

I differ with traditional interpreters of the Genesis story in this respect: they seem to think that the role of Man in Eden should have been one of trust - trust and obey - while I see it as inevitably of testing, for there is no other way for Man to know who he is than by testing the very One who has been responsible for his own being what he is, so if the Man is to discover who he himself is, he must find out who God is.

As this little Man discovers something about his Creator/Father, what sort of Father this God is, he discovers his own boundaries; now he learns that while God will give him rather wide privileges - yes he can eat of all the trees in the garden - he learns that God will not allow him full rein to do as he pleases. God will put some restriction on him. May be just to let him know that there is a distance between them. That God controls and Man has only a delegated control over things. Hence the prohibition. DON'T EAT THAT ONE.

Now we are at the core of the Creation Myth. Man has free rein in the garden ...EXCEPT. And that single exception is just what Man must grasp, if he is to discover himself in relation to, his Creator/Father. It is the test, test of God, consequently test of Man. But it is the right test. For Man wants to know if God means what He says And he finds that God does mean it. But the "mean" is not what he thinks it is because "to die" is something he cannot understand when he has not yet lived.

But the test did reveal to Man that God is Power, and that Power is capable of hurting him. And this revelation taught him that he, Man really had Power, but a lesser Power. Until he could attain a stature matching that of God, it would be a lesser Power, but the Knowledge of Good and Evil put him in position to try for that Power which he recognized to be in God now.

And amazingly, but really quite naturally, in discovering the Knowledge of Good and Evil, he learned that he had done the wrong thing. He had challenged the Superior Power, who now lowered the beam on him, kicked him out of that cool and pleasant garden, out onto the desert of rocks and thorns, with no possibility of return to the garden of innocence.

But if anybody thinks this is going to humble Man into submission to that Power, he has failed to notice that the very core of Man's being is that he has the Power which continually drives him to challenge God for the place of equality on the throne. So we have not yet heard the end of the story. Just the Genesis.

So Man has discovered something about himself now. At the very moment when he gains the knowledge of Good and Evil, which makes him truly like God, he discovers that he has made a blunder, done the wrong thing, which in this case amounts to choosing the Evil. It was inevitable.

As strange as it may seem to the Reader, here is Man's Godlikeness. For God has made this same discovery; in making Man in His image, and then setting a prohibition on him, God has jeopardized His own throne.

It is by telling Man that he must not eat this fruit, that God makes certain that Man will eat it. And at the same time He puts Himself in the position of having to throw Man out of the Garden, lest he do even more damage by eating the fruit of the Tree of Life, and gaining that other divine prerogative, Immortality. But, the joke is on God. Man has already got the key to immortality because he has learned that he can reproduce himself, and it is in this that the next face off is determined.

For Man now, in the persons of the two brothers, Cain and Abel, who are on the scene because Adam has found this secret, attempt to placate the offended God, and each tries to ingratiate himself to that God, and in doing so, they put God in the position of having to make a choice, to show favor to one of them. This makes the unfavored one angry; he kills the favored one, and in turn is thrown upon the mercy of the very God who rejected his offering. He has also put God on the spot, for God now must protect him from the vengeance that others may wreak on him for what he has done. And all because of God.

So Man's attempt to placate and propitiate God ends in failure. Worse than failure. It complicates matters for both God and Man. And matters now go from bad to worse; the whole human race is so badly off center that God decides to destroy the whole batch. But this poses a problem for God because it not only implies that God has made a mistake in the Creation of Man; it says He is not able to control His Creation. So what good is His Power if He must admit defeat? He settles for a partial destruction. He will save ONE MAN, NOAH.

And God now stakes the future of His Creation on this ONE MAN, NOAH, enters into an alliance with him, and destroys all the others. That is the story of THE FLOOD.

Again, as in the Creation story, the Flood story is not unique. It may be a little different from the other Flood Myths in other parts of the world, but it is essentially the same: God chooses one man, Noah, forms an alliance with him against all the others, and destroys His original Creation with a Flood.

What is of real importance to us in the Flood Myth is that it is an admission of failure on God's part, as well as one of judgment on the way Man has handled his Knowledge of Good and Evil. Knowing both, Man has chosen Evil. Indeed, knowing both only because he has chosen Evil. But God, having the supreme Power, has chosen to use it to destroy, rather than to redeem Man. That is to say, God, knowing both Good and Evil, has chosen to use His Power to do Evil. And it is only in retrospect, when the Flood is past, that God repents of His Evil.

At this point it is necessary to face the dual nature of both God and Man as both God and Man are revealed to us in Genesis. Creation and Destruction. Good and Evil. But the Flood Myth is so big that it must be repeated in the legendary tales of the nation Israel. It is to be found again in the story of Joseph, the favored son of Jacob. Here the moral is simply inverted, and the result is different, but it is the same story. One is chosen, the others cast aside.

Again, it is repeated in the story of David, son of Jesse, who is chosen to be King of Israel while his brothers sink into oblivion. Again, the same story, God striking a bargain with His Chosen One. Ultimately, it is repeated in the story of Jesus called the Christ, God's very own Chosen Son. But that can wait for its proper place in the story. Now the whole world is under water, and we have to wait to see whether this alliance between God and Noah is going to work out. And I have to tell you, dear Reader, that the new beginning is no better than the original. In fact, Noah gets drunk and brings about a new division among the Sons of Men because he shows special disfavor to the one who uncovers his shame.

The seed of ambition, though, is still there in Man, and next we will see it come to flower in the building of the Tower of Babel. In this Myth of the Tower, Man takes the initiative in reaching for God's place by his own efforts. If Heaven is the abode of God, then the way to get there is obvious: build a tower that will reach to Heaven. Then just walk right in and announce that you have come to stay and to share in the amenities of Deity, Power being the main one.

So the Men with this common goal got together and started building their tower. We are not told how far they got, and it does not matter. What does matter is that when their objective became obvious, God took action because they had become a threat to His position as the Supreme Power in both Heaven and Earth, so He confused their tongues, and all communication between them ceased, and as a consequence, work on the Tower ceased.

Greek mythology has a counterpart: Zeus the High God created Man both Male and Female in one being called Androgenes, who was round, which is the shape of perfection. But when Zeus looked at this Perfect Creation, He saw that Androgenes was a threat to him. "Why, this fellow could roll right up to the top of Mount Olympus and take over. There is no limit to what this Male/Female round Man could do. He could certainly upset the balance of Power on Mount Olympus. Something has to be done about Him/Her."

So Zeus took in hand a God sized sword, and he brought the blade down on Androgenes, slicing Him/ Her into halves. One half rolled to the left as Man; the other half rolled to the right, as Woman. Or maybe it was the other way; it does not matter, for now Man and Woman were separated, and they had a problem which became more important and more insistent, far more immediate than taking over the ambrosia bowl on Mount Olympus. The problem was to get back together. This proved to be a task of such monumental size and complexity that the two have been busy at it ever since. And Zeus reigns supreme on his throne.

Certainly, God's blow at the communications system of the men on the Tower was as effective as Zeus' blow at the head of Androgenes. At any rate, men are still trying to talk with one another, and they are still just talking at one another. It may help some if all peoples speak English, but it does not solve the problem because we don't all mean the same thing with the words we use. Nor do we all hear the same thing when the same words are used. So we end with a babble of voices and God is safe on his throne in Heaven.

So we have here another failure on Man's part to gain equality with God. God has deliberately foiled Man's attempt to storm Heaven, has sent babbling Man sprawling upon the Earth, to lick his wounds, and to gather his forces for another attempt. God is safe in His inviolable Heaven, and all is not well with Man on the Earth. But Man has not given up the struggle.

And the next move on the giant chess board will be made by God Himself. He will choose a Man who seems to hold more promise than anyone else. And He will train up this Man for a special role. ENTER ABRAHAM.

Abraham is not quite a mythic figure; yet he is too big for a mere historical one. He is legendary. The Father of three great religious faiths. So he certainly figures big with God. But just what is his role in this drama? God chose Abraham out of the whole of Mankind, and God proposed to work through Abraham to have an effect on the whole of Mankind. This is certainly a definite advance over the experiment with Noah. He is not going to flood the Earth again. He is not going to bowl over towers. Nor throw Man out of the Garden. God is going to make a new approach. What is it?

This time God will work from within. One Man, Abraham, will spark the movement of Mankind toward the desired destiny of a special relationship with God. What is different here as we move from the mythic to the legendary era of the struggle is that the Man Abraham is now the Father, so he actually represents God among Men.

Does this mean, then, that God has decided to voluntarily share His Power with Man? Perhaps. But God is going to work through a representative, Father Abraham, and the Men who come into this Power sharing, Divinity sharing relationship with God, will do so by becoming the Seed of Abraham.

Another way of putting it is that God is working through Abraham to draw Men to Himself. But He strikes an obstacle in Abraham's nephew Lot who settles in the Sodom/Gomorrah region, and Lot's wife likes the society there. God sends messengers to warn these rebellious children but they don't heed the message. In fact, they would violate the messengers, so God destroys the cities of Sodom and Gomorrah, after giving Lot a chance to escape, but Lot's wife looks back and is turned to a pillar of salt. So we are back into Myth again. And it is none other than the Myth of the Garden of Eden, with Adam and Eve and the serpent, only it now has a different twist, in that Lot escapes, but into anonymity because he is no longer needed for the story.

But what is the myth telling us? That Man, having got the secrets of the Garden, especially the one about Sex and eternal Life, is now experimenting, still hoping to gain that place beside God Himself.

For is not fertility the real secret of the gods? It is indeed, the secret of Life on Earth. God, on the other hand, the God who chose Abraham, and will work out His own plan through him, disapproves Man running wild with this secret, and He does to Sodom and Gomorrah, and to Lot's wife, what He did to the race of giants with the Flood. God is narrowing His focus to Abraham and his Seed. And we are gaining an insight to what God's purpose is. He is going to grow Him a race of people who will reflect His character, become a reflection of His own Face in the world, so that the great unwashed race of men can see what He is about, see the divine purpose in God's Chosen, Abraham's Seed.

But Abraham was making some interesting discoveries about this God who had chosen him, and these were discoveries which would ultimately determine the moral fibre of the Man who would achieve the place beside his God. And the first was in the area of SEX. Abraham got into trouble by passing off his wife Sara as his sister on the Pharoah in Egypt. And the second discovery he made was in his attempt to sacrifice his son Isaac to God as a palliative measure which proved to be entirely unsatisfactory and unacceptable as a substitute for character.

Both of these experiments, with the resulting lessons learned, would find expression in the eighth century B.C. prophets who asked what God requires of Man, then answered their own question by saying that sacrifice won't cut it, for God requires justice, mercy and humility. That is to say, CHARACTER reflective of what they hope to find in God, with an attitude that will be acceptable to such a God.

In that trade off deal with Pharoah, in which Sara was the pawn, Abraham had learned that this gift of SEX was not to be played around with as a bargaining tool. The Sodom/Gomorrah lesson was even stronger. Abuse this gift at great peril to your life. And the Isaac sacrifice experiment clinched it; God was serious about Life, and Abraham had better be serious too, if he hoped to stand beside God in the long line of Life stretching into the future.

Obviously then, if God and Man are to get together, it is necessary that Man learn what is the necessary character of both God and Man. In other words, if we are to know who God Is, we have to know What God requires of Man in order for Man to achieve his divine destiny. And if we are to know What Man is to Become, we have to find it in God's Face.

Somewhere between Abraham and Jesus the idea of Israel, composed of Abraham's seed as God's son, and the Messianic concept of the Son of Man as the full flowering of that special relationship, came into the Israelite self concept so when Jesus of Nazareth came to herald the Kingdom of God as an immanent reality among men, he took for himself the title Son of Man. When he rode in triumph into Jerusalem, he was proclaimed the Son of David. And the religious leaders accused him of believing himself the Son of God. But except in the Gospel of John, which is a full blown philosophy/theology written long after his death, and apparently independent of the synoptic gospels, Jesus is always The Son of Man, and this term carries the full weight of all Messianic hopes and fulfillment.

The implications of this for the full blown picture of Man are far reaching, and what they lack in touching Heaven, the fourth Gospel and the letters attributed to John, fill out with Man in Christ Jesus becoming identical with the Son who is identical with the Father, which is to say that God and Man have become One in Christ Jesus.

This is why the religious leaders rejected and killed him; it is also why the little people followed him and declared him the Risen Son who has united with the Father to be the Savior of Man.

But in the Prologue to John's Gospel we are taken back to the Creation, and we are told that this Man is that Creative word of God that brought everything into being, and is now revealed in the flesh as Jesus of Nazareth, in whom the very glory of God may be seen. Then, in the letter, I John 2:1,2, the writer says that when we look on His Face and see Him revealed to us for what He is, then we become like Him, so the end of Creation is achieved. God has been revealed in Man and Man is now identified with God.

Man now has the Power which is the essence of God, and he will be able to do all the things he has seen In Jesus as expression of that divine Power. Because the Man who has now identified with Him has now been endowed with His own being, and is not a mere mirror image, but the reality.

Jesus of Nazareth is a historical figure who was hanged for his offense against Judaism and Rome, but there is no way to get around the mythical aspect of the Christ who was born of a virgin, performed miracles, and was raised from the dead and ascended into Heaven. So in Christ Jesus the ultimate Creation Myth is seen, for here God and Man meet on the plane of history, indeed at the very dawn of history in a new Creation, the Man in Christ Jesus, who is the Real Man with the Power to do all things, for Heaven has come to Earth, the Kingdom of Heaven has come on Earth. And Man, the New

Creation, is born and rules on Earth. The Creation Myth has become historical reality.

In Jesus Christ we have the Ultimate Myth, avatar and apotheosis. God becomes Man; Man becomes God.

EPILOGUE

Now I have told You these thirty stories from the Book. And one from outside the Book. From the Creation of Man to his exaltation. From Man's appearance on this Earth as a Babe in Eden to the Babe in Bethlehem Who is the Son of Man.

From his discovery of Good and Evil to the triumph of Good over Evil. From Adam in Eden to the Man in Christ.

In my wonderment I have let my imagination soar at times come again to Earth for strength. I hope I have rightly discerned the Mind of God in these Conversations. And I hope I have drawn your mind in them too.

ABOUT THE AUTHOR

I write; therefore I am. I write about interesting and eccentric people. And goats. My first published book was AND THE GOAT CRIED. His tears moved me deeply and I wrote THE GOAT ALSO LAUGHED. I wrote the ALFIE STORIES because I am Alfie and being a boy was a great adventure.

I earned a doctorate in Biblical Theology and wrote THE TELEVANGELIST, THE SINNER MESSIAH, then balanced them off with THE DAY CHRIST CAME BACK. Politics interests me. I wrote JAY CEE about the Presidency. Social issues intrigue me; I wrote IN THE TOBACCO PATCH.

Joseph Campbell nudged my interest in mythology; I wrote THE MARRIAGE MYTH and OEDIPUS REVISITED. Both Love and War interest me. I wrote FOR LOVE OF LEANDER and NO GREATER LOVE. But we got into the Persian Gulf War, and I wrote THE DEVIL AND TOM WALKER. Then this one, and I wrote TERROR! TERROR! & TOM WALKER TWO.

But I find God the most interesting of all. So here I give you MY CONVERSATIONS WITH GOD. I was filled with wonder at all He had to say to me, once I started asking Him questions about the characters He has created and chosen to do things in His world. I bet you will be too once you visit the Tree of Knowledge of Good and Evil, and read about the struggle between Good and Evil on the cross of Jesus.

I had to write eighteen other books before God would give me this assignment, but He has promised me another one if I get this one right. He is very strict about getting it right, and He keeps me wondering what's next, but if this one goes over well with Him, you can watch for THE SHELLMAN STORY. That's the one in which I got hanged.

Printed in the United States
69891LV00004B/154-162